POWER AND ENERGY

HISTORY OF INVENTION

POWER AND ENERGY

Chris Woodford

Facts On File, Inc.

Facts On File, Inc.
132 West 31st Street
New York, NY 10001

Library of Congress Cataloging-in-Publication Data

Woodford, Chris
    Power and energy / Chris Woodford.
       p. cm.
    Summary: Reviews the history of power and energy inventions, from the dawn of civilization to the present, including the first machines, steam and electric engines, and the incandescent lightbulb.
    Includes bibliographical references and index.
    ISBN 0-8160-5440-1
    1. Power (Mechanics)—History—Juvenile literature.
2. Power resources—History—Juvenile literature.
[1. Power (Mechanics)—History. 2. Power Resources
—History.] I. Title.

TJ163.95.W66 2004
621.042—dc22

                                    2003013449

Facts On File books are available at special discounts when purchased in bulk quantities for businesses, associations, institutions, or sales promotions. Please call our Special Sales Department in New York at (212) 967-8800 or (800) 322-8755.

You can find Facts On File on the World Wide Web at
http://www.factsonfile.com

For The Brown Reference Group plc:
Project Editor: Tom Jackson
Design: Bradbury and Williams
Picture Research: Becky Cox
Managing Editor: Bridget Giles
Consultant: Dr. Donald R. Franceschetti, Distinguished
    Service Professor, University of Memphis, Tennessee.

Printed and bound in Singapore

10 9 8 7 6 5 4 3 2 1

CONTENTS

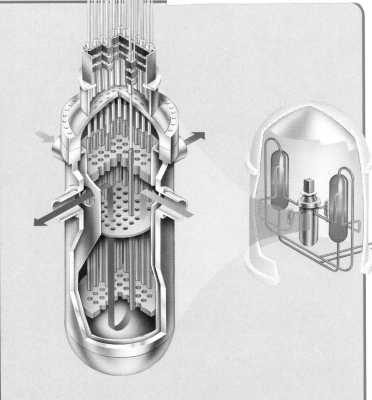

THE WORLD OF ENERGY

Almost everything that happens on our planet requires energy of some kind. Plants need energy to grow, automobiles need energy to power their engines, and people need energy to live and to make things. Energy comes in many forms, such as heat, light, or motion: Machines are devices that convert one source of energy into different forms.

The power that reaches our planet from the Sun every second of every day is roughly the same as the energy in the oil carried by six gigantic tanker ships. A square of Earth's surface a little bigger than a person's two feet receives roughly the same amount of light

and heat from the Sun as a table lamp would provide. Imagine Earth's surface covered in table lamps and you'll have some idea just how much energy the Sun sends in our direction.

Talking of *energy* suggests that it comes in only one form. In fact, there are many different types of energy, and they can usually be converted from one to the other. The Sun beams a mixture of light and heat energy toward Earth. Animals use the heat to keep warm, while plants use the light to grow through a chemical reaction called *photosynthesis*. The energy that plants store does not disappear,

Everything can be described in terms of energy. The flowers in the foreground are receiving energy from sunlight. The car speeds along using energy released from burning fuel. As with the plants, the energy in the fuel originally came from the Sun.

however. Millions of years after they die, plants might turn into fossils and then become energy-rich coal or peat. In the same way, tiny sea organisms called plankton can turn into oil. Fossil fuels such as peat, coal, and oil contain chemical energy that can be burned in engines to produce mechanical energy—the energy that makes a machine work. Inside power plants, engines spin huge generators to make electrical energy, better known as electricity.

ENERGY, WORK, AND FORCE

In everyday life, people think of energy as something that gives them the "get-up-and-go" to do things like going to school or work. Energy is much the same in science. To a scientist, energy is the ability to do work. Work means exerting a force on object over a distance.

A force is a push or pull on an object that causes it to move or change its direction. One force that is acting all the time is gravity. This is the force of Earth pulling you and everything else toward it. The force of gravity acting on an object is called its weight. To lift anything, you have to apply a force that is greater than its weight, and this requires giving it more energy.

By doing work, such as pushing a car, you are adding energy to the car. This energy may come from your muscles or from an engine, and the more work you do the more energy is required. It takes more work, for example, to move a truck than a car, and more work is needed to move the same car over a longer distance.

The energy is not lost or used up as the work is done. Instead it is converted into another form. If you pushed a car up a hill and then let go, it would roll back down to

Skateboarders must control the forces acting on their board to ride along, change direction, and perform tricks.

the bottom again. As you push the car up the hill, it stores some of the energy. This energy is called potential energy, since it gives the car the potential to do work in the future, such as roll down the hill. Any kind of stored energy is potential energy. When you charge a cell phone battery, you are storing potential energy in an electrical form that you can draw on later when the phone is turned on.

A little of the energy is always turned into heat caused by friction (objects rubbing together), but most of the work done is converted into potential energy. The higher up the hill you push the car, and the longer you charge up the cell phone, therefore, the more potential energy they receive.

CREATE NOR DESTROY

It is impossible to make energy out of thin air or to make it disappear completely. All we can do is change it from one form into another. This idea is called the conservation of energy, and it was first figured out by British physicist James Prescott Joule (1818–89). Suppose you make a cup of coffee. The water you use needs to be hot. In other words, it needs heat energy. That comes from boiling a kettle, which increases the heat energy in the water using electrical energy. The electrical energy, in turn, comes from a power plant that has burned a certain amount of coal, oil, or another fuel. Millions of

People and society

Perpetual Motion

All machines need a supply of energy to run. Without it they will grind to a halt. For many years, inventors have tried to produce so-called perpetual motion machines that can go on working forever without a supply of energy. However, this is impossible, and anyone who tried simply did not understand energy. A machine from 1661 (above) was meant to use a waterwheel to drive gears. The gears were to raise water, which then powered the wheel. The designer did not understand that some of the energy used to turn the components would be converted into heat. The heat would be produced as the gears rubbed against each other, in the same way as your hands warm up when you rub them together. The heat energy is lost, and the machine's motion gradually begins to slow down.

Frauds tried to convince people that perpetual motion was possible. In 1813, Charles Redheffer built a box of gears that he said would turn all by themselves. The steamboat pioneer Robert Fulton (1765–1815) unmasked the fraud, when he found the machine was being secretly driven by a cord. He followed the cord to another room and found an old man turning a handle that drove Redheffer's machine.

years ago, the energy in that fuel originally came from the Sun. And the Sun produces its energy from nuclear fusion reactions. So, in a way, the coffee you drink is nuclear powered!

ENERGY AND ELECTRICITY
One of the problems with energy is that it is not always there when you need it. In the modern world, people do not want to go out and gather firewood every time they need to cook a meal, although this is how many people in developing countries still live their lives. People also do not want to have to burn candles to light their homes. Instead, they want to simply turn on the stove and the electric lights and get their energy delivered right away.

How things work

Newton's Laws

Modern understanding of energy and force began with English physicist Isaac Newton (1643–1727). Newton's work started a scientific revolution when people finally understood that the world around them could be explained by a handful of simple physical laws.

Newton (right) is best remembered for his law of gravity. This explains how the same force that causes objects to fall to the ground when close to Earth's surface is also responsible for the way Earth and the other planets move around the Sun.

Newton also figured out three important laws that show how forces make things happen in the universe. Newton's laws of motion, as these are known, still form the basis of modern physics almost 300 years after he first proposed them.

Newton's first law describes *inertia*. It says that an object will stay still or keep moving along at a steady speed unless a force acts on it. If you stand on a skateboard, you will not move until you push off against the sidewalk. Newton's second law says that an object will accelerate (speed up) or change direction while a force is acting on it. If you are on a skateboard, it is the force from your kick against the sidewalk that makes the skateboard accelerate. The third law says that if a force acts on an object, there is always an opposite force produced by the object. When you kick backward against the sidewalk, it is the force of the sidewalk pushing against the sole of your shoe that makes the skateboard move.

Skiers illustrate the idea behind potential energy. Those on the chairlift are increasing their potential energy as they climb up the slope. At the top, skiers release this potential energy as they begin to slide down to the bottom.

Grand Coulee Dam, Washington, holds back the water of the Columbia River. As the water flows through the dam on its way to the sea, large fanlike turbines and generators convert the water's energy into electricity.

Electricity is the most versatile energy of all, because it can be stored, transmitted from place to place, and turned into just about any other kind of energy by a wide range of electrical appliances. Electricity gives us flexibility in how we use energy.

For example, at the Grand Coulee Dam in Washington State, huge amounts of electrical energy are produced by a hydroelectric plant that extracts movement energy from the waters of the Columbia River. Electricity made here and by Washington's other dams is supplied to 11 other states. When it reaches consumers, it can be used in any number of different ways, from heating stoves to operating televisions, and from powering computers to driving subway trains.

No one ever invented electricity, it was always there. But the inventors who harnessed its power have revolutionized the modern world by making it possible for us to use energy whenever and wherever we need it.

THE FIRST MACHINES

The history of civilization is a history of human technology. It is the story of the inventions people have developed to make life easier. Even before people learned to control fire, they had developed simple tools. The very earliest tools, such as hand axes and levers, are even older than modern humans. These first machines were used by humanlike creatures that came before us.

WHAT ARE MACHINES?
It is often hard for people to think of many of these ancient inventions as machines at all.

To us, a machine is something like a railroad locomotive or a vacuum cleaner. A machine can be defined more precisely, however. It is any device that changes the size of a force or alters the direction in which it is applied. This means a hammer is a machine, because it increases the force with which you can bang a nail into the wall. A wheel is also a machine, because it reduces the force you need to push something along. And a knife is a machine, because it focuses the force you use to cut things. Just about every machine that has ever been invented falls

This horse-drawn plow from the early 19th century is a combination of two simple machines. The wheels on the side act like levers to make it easier to move the heavy plow forward. The metal blade of the plow acts like a wedge, multiplying the plow's pushing force so it cuts into the soil.

Archimedes Screw

Greek thinker Archimedes (287–212 B.C.E.) is best remembered for explaining buoyancy—the way things float in water. But he also pioneered a great deal of modern mathematics and invented a number of useful machines. One of these is the Archimedes screw, a simple machine that can move liquids or powders (above, being used for irrigation). It looks like a huge drill bit fixed snugly inside a large pipe. As it slowly rotates, the thread of the screw pulls liquid or powder from one end of the pipe to the other. The Archimedes screw was one of the first water pumps, and is still widely used today.

into one of five basic types. These are the lever, the wheel and axle, the pulley, the inclined plane or wedge, and the screw.

FROM MACHINES TO TOOLS

The earliest tools date back to 2.5 million years ago. This period is known as the Stone Age because people used stone to make many of their tools. They chipped sharp edges into hand-sized rocks to make crude cutters and choppers. The sharpened edges work like a wedge to multiply the force from a person's hand. Stone-Age tools were also made from other things. For example, antlers was used to make a pick for digging up the ground. This tool was a combination of two machines: The handle behaved like a lever, while the point was a wedge.

Other machines date from the Bronze Age, which started between 4500 and 2000 B.C.E. in different parts of the world. This was the time when people learned how to mix copper and tin to make a tough alloy known as bronze. Not everything invented at this time was made from bronze, however. Stone, wood, bone, and other materials remained important. Many Bronze Age machines had some connection with agriculture. Shears were invented around 4500 B.C.E., and the plow was another Bronze-Age development.

One of the most important inventions of all time, the wheel and axle, also dates from this period. It was invented around

How Good is a Machine?

There are two ways of measuring how well a machine does its job—mechanical advantage or efficiency. The mechanical advantage of a machine is the amount by which it multiplies a force. A pulley with four ropes and a 5-ton (4.5-metric ton) weight can lift a 20-ton (18 metric-ton) load. The effort needed to lift the weight is four times less than the load, so the mechanical advantage is four.

The efficiency of a machine compares the amount of work it does to the energy it consumes. Efficiency is usually expressed as a percentage. Something that is completely efficient would convert all the energy it takes in into useful work; in other words, it would be 100 percent efficient. In practice, no machine is ever that good. Perhaps the most efficient machines are water turbines in hydroelectric plants. They are 90 percent efficient, removing all but 10 percent of the energy from the water.

A horse-powered pulley system is used to unload a coal barge. The pulleys multiply the force of the horse, but the horse must walk many times farther than the buckets are raised.

3500 B.C.E. in Mesopotamia (the land between the Tigris and Euphrates Rivers now in Iraq).

EGYPTIAN ADVANCES

In drier parts of the Middle East, the ancient Egyptians invented machines to supply water to their crops. One of the devices they

developed was the *shaduf*, a water-raising machine that looks a bit like a see-saw, only with a bucket on one end and a counterweight at the other. Using a shaduf, which is a type of lever, a person can easily raise heavy buckets of water several feet in the air to water crops growing on different levels. The Egyptians were also the first people to master the art of using machines to build large-scale structures. Although they had wheels and axles, Egyptian construction engineers did not make use of pulleys to raise heavy objects. Instead they relied on a huge workforce to heave blocks of stone into place. Pulleys date from 800 B.C.E. They were first used in what is now northern Iraq.

THE GREEKS AND ROMANS

The Greeks were the first people to understand the science behind machines. Indeed, the ancient Greeks gave us the word *machine* from their word *mechane*, which means "device." Greek inventor Hero of Alexandria set out the theory behind the five basic machines in the first century. As well as developing the world's first steam engine, Hero also invented many other mechanical devices, including some driven by compressed air. These included an automatic doorbell and another device that could open the doors of a temple using hot air. The word *automatic* also comes from Greek: *Automata* were toys that appeared to move by themselves.

The shaduf is a simple machine used for raising water from rivers. It has a bucket suspended from a long arm that is pivoted near one end. On the other side of the pivot to the bucket, is a heavy weight. This weight raises the bucket of water. The arm multiplies the force produced by the weight, making it easier to lift large amounts of water.

long arm

counterweight

pivot

bucket

Construction Machines

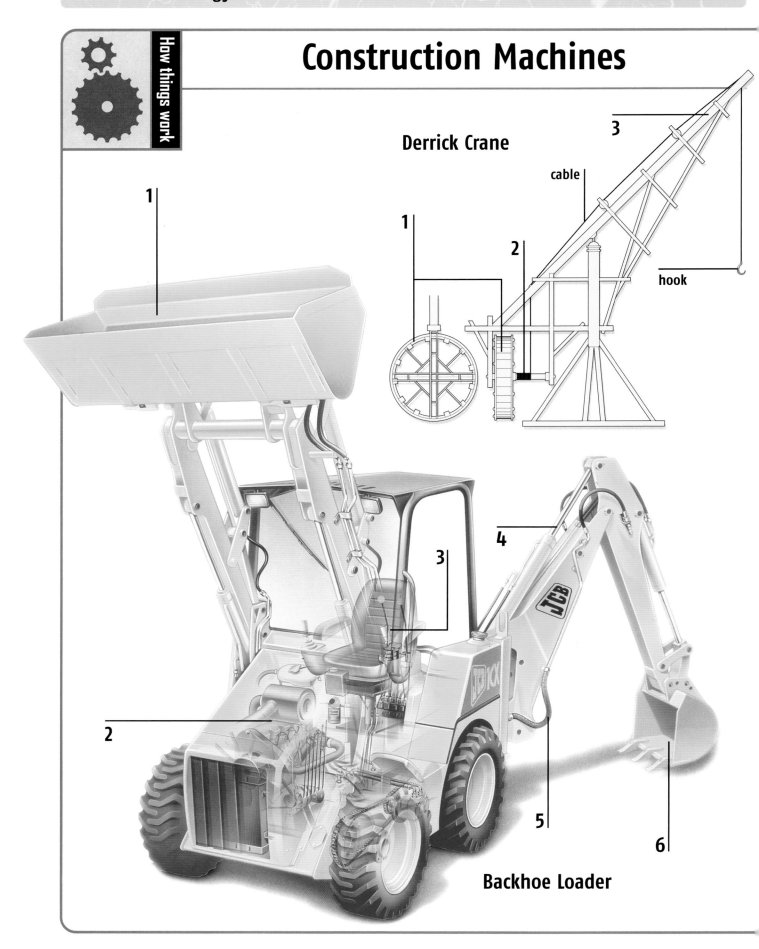

Derrick Crane

cable

hook

1

2

3

1

2

3

4

5

6

Backhoe Loader

People have always needed to lift heavy objects. There is a limit to how much can be done by muscle power alone, and machines have made construction much easier. Although no evidence remains, historians believe many ancient people used A-frames and ramps to raise heavy monuments. Cranes were invented 2,000 years ago.

Derrick Crane

This crane was first used in Italy in the 15th century. It was based on designs used by the Romans.

1. The crane was powered by people moving in the treadmill.

2. The treadmill wound the cable around a simple winch.

3. The cable ran along a movable arm called the jib.

Backhoe Loader

Backhoe loaders are versatile modern machines used on construction sites. They can dig holes and carry loads.

1. The front bucket is used for scooping up loose earth or rubble.

2. The engine provides power for both the arms and drives the wheels.

3. The machine is controlled from the driver's cab.

4. Both the arms are moved by hydraulic (liquid-filled) pistons. These move when liquids are pumped into them.

5. Hydraulic liquid is pumped around the machine through thick hoses.

6. The rear bucket, or backhoe, is used for digging holes.

Many modern inventions are just highly developed versions of the five basic machines. For example, this drill is a wedge that cuts through hard surfaces. The drill is pneumatic. This means that the up-and-down motion of the wedge is produced by compressed air.

The Romans took over as the dominant power in Europe after the Greeks. They built an empire between 27 B.C.E. and 395 C.E. and invented machines, such as human-powered cranes, to help them do it. Roman carpenters were well-equipped with tools such as drills, lathes, saws, and axes, and their blacksmiths had hammers, tongs, and anvils. They used this equipment to develop a range of both wooden and metal machines. They made advances in machines that produced rotary (round-and-round) motion and began to use the power of flowing water to drive machines.

SIMPLE MACHINES

Machines make things easier for us. They do this in two ways. They may change the size of a force, generally increasing it, but on occasion reducing it. Other machines redirect the force so it acts in another way. Although most familiar machines perform both of these roles, we can describe how they work in terms of five simple machines: the lever, the wheel and axle, the pulley, the wedge, and the screw.

At first sight, simple machines like this may seem to break one of the most basic laws of physics: They seem to make it possible to do the same amount of work with less energy. In fact, just as much energy is needed to do a job whether a machine is used or not. Machines reduce the effort needed to do work, not the energy. It takes just as much energy to push a car up a ramp as to lift it straight upward. The work seems easier, but it takes longer. Less force is needed with a ramp, but the force must be used over a greater distance. The work done and the energy needed are the same in both cases.

Many everyday objects are simple machines or combinations of them. For example, tongs are two levers joined together. Wrenches are also simple levers. Like tongs, shears are two levers joined together. Instead of gripping objects, however, the wedge-shaped blades cut through them. Adjustable wrenches also use a screw to move the jaws.

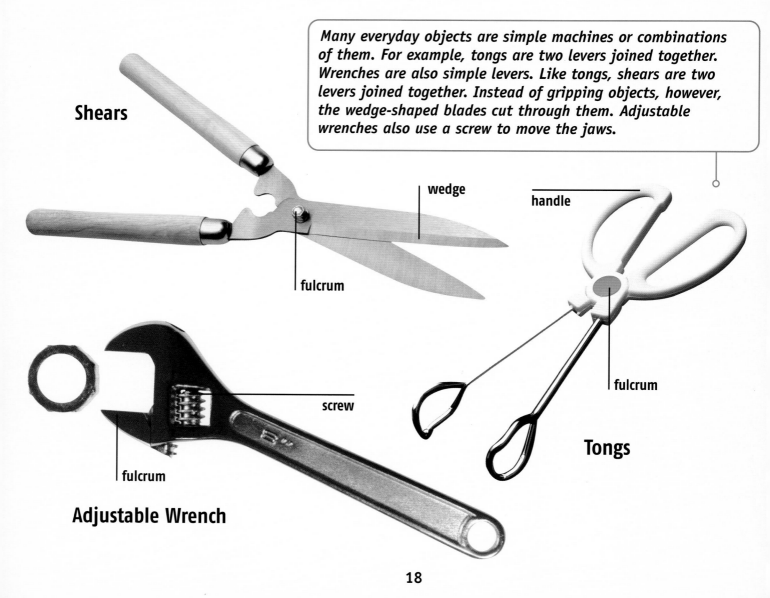

Shears

wedge

fulcrum

handle

fulcrum

screw

fulcrum

Adjustable Wrench

Tongs

Lever

A lever is a rigid bar that changes a small force at one end, known as the effort, into a larger force, known as the load, at the other end using a pivot-point called a fulcrum. By varying the position of the fulcrum, it is possible to lift bigger or smaller loads with more or less effort. Examples of levers include crowbars, see-saws, tongs, and scissors.

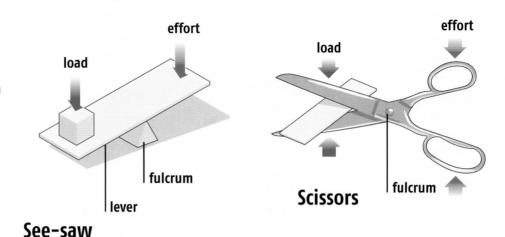

See-saw

Scissors

Wheel and Axle

A wheel and axle is a kind of rotating lever in which the axle works as the fulcrum. This is why it is much easier to push a heavy cart if it has big wheels. When you shove the cart forward, the pushing force (the effort) is multiplied by the large wheels into a much bigger force (the load) at the axle.

A pulley is a pair of wheels and axles connected together by a number of ropes. The more ropes there are, the less the effort needed to lift the load. The number of ropes is equal to the mechanical advantage of a pulley.

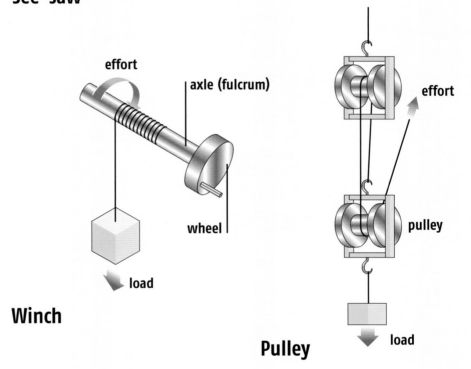

Winch

Pulley

Inclined Planes

An inclined plane can be used as a ramp to make it easier to lift things. Much less effort is needed to push a heavy weight up a ramp than to lift it straight up.

Inclined planes can also be used as wedges, for example, to help split firewood. When the hammer strikes the thick end of the wedge, its force is multiplied greatly at the thin end. Blades are also examples of wedges.

A screw is like an inclined plane wrapped around an axle. The handle of a screw is also usually a lever.

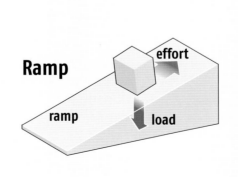

Ramp

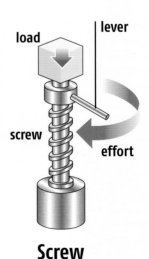

Screw

THE POWER OF THE WHEEL

Ancient civilizations went a long way with simple machines, such as levers and ramps. But another invention—the wheel—would take them much farther. Wooden wheels revolutionized pottery and transportation and made it possible for people to harness the power of nature in important new ways.

Metal wheels, which were developed much later, were more useful. As well as being fitted to stronger and faster vehicles, metal wheels were used in devices for telling the time, measuring things very accurately, and even finding the way across the ocean. Few innovations have changed society quite so much as the wheel.

THE BIRTH OF WHEEL POWER
No one knows exactly when the wheel was invented. The idea of powering things that moved around and around, instead of back and forth, seems to have developed during the Stone Age, more than two million years ago. This was when people invented the drill and the lathe, two simple tools that are still used today. Early drills and lathes were sharp sticks that were spun back and forth by a string attached to a bow. Unlike wheels, they did not always spin in the same direction, but turned first one way and then the other.

Today, we think of wheels in connection with transportation, but they were first used for

Slaves are forced to power a treadmill at an 18th-century sugar plantation in the Caribbean. Treadmills powered by people or livestock were the first engines.

Gear Wheels

A gear is a pair of wheels with teeth, or sprockets, that mesh (join) to multiply the force or speed with which a machine is turning. If two identical gears mesh together (1), both turn with the same speed and the same force. They also turn in opposing directions. A third wheel, called an idler, has to be added between the two wheels if they both need to rotate in the same direction (2). Something different happens when gear wheels have different numbers of teeth to each other. When a gear wheel drives a smaller one with half as many teeth (3), the smaller wheel makes twice the number of turns as the larger one. The second wheel also turns with half as much torque (twisting force) than the first wheel. In other words, a gear that doubles the speed halves the force. The opposite is also true. If the first wheel drives a larger wheel with twice as many teeth (4), the speed is halved but the force is doubled.

Bicycles and other vehicles make the most of gears. When going uphill, the gear attached to the pedal drives a larger gear wheel that has more teeth. This means the pedals turn more often than

the bicycle wheels, but the wheels push the bike with greater force. In other words, the gears act like force multipliers. On the flat, the pedal drives a much smaller gear wheel that has fewer teeth. The smaller gear wheel has to turn around more often to keep up with the pedals, so the bicycle wheels turn more quickly than the pedals. On level roads, gears work as speed multipliers to make a bicycle go faster.

1 sprocket

speed

torque

2

3 central idler

speed

torque

4

speed

torque

drive wheel

improving the quality of pots and bowls. Potters kicked a wheel around with their feet to make circular items. It was not until about 3500 B.C.E., in the ancient Middle East, that wheels were incorporated into carts. The first wheels were completely solid pieces of wood, which made them very sturdy but also very heavy. It took about 1,500 years for people to transform the solid wheel into a much lighter wheel with spokes that is still commonly used today.

GEARS IN ANCIENT GREECE

Wheels and axles were among the simple machines that the Greek engineer Hero of Alexandria described 2,000 years ago. Like many other Greek inventors, Hero devised a number of inventions based on the wheel. They included the *hodometer*, a large wheel attached to a stick that can be used to measure distances. Other Greek inventors built the first waterwheels. Unlike their more modern counterparts, these wheels were held flat in the water.

The Greeks' biggest innovation in rotary power was the invention of gears with teeth. These wheels can increase the speed or force of a rotating machine. Although it is unclear who invented gears, they were described by the great thinker Aristotle (384–322 B.C.E.) and were used by many Greek inventors. Ctesibius of Alexandria, for example, is thought to have built a water-driven clock which used gears in 150 B.C.E. Hero of

Cams and Cranks

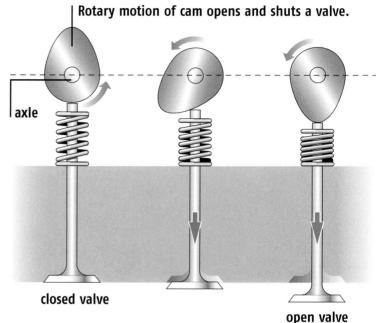

Rotary motion of cam opens and shuts a valve.

axle

closed valve

open valve

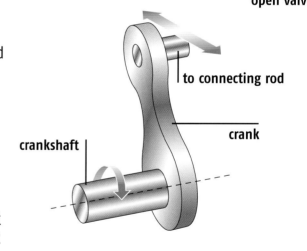

to connecting rod

crank

crankshaft

Windmills and waterwheels generate rotary power, but machines often need to make pushing-and-pulling forces (known as reciprocating motion) instead. Two inventions—the cam and the crankshaft—made it possible to convert rotary motion into reciprocating motion and back again.

The cam is an egg-shaped wheel that turns around on an axle. If something like a beam or a piston rests on top of the cam, it moves up and down as the cam moves around and around. This converts the rotary motion of the cam into up-and-down reciprocating motion in the connected piston. Inside automobile engines, cams are used to control the valves that open and close to let air and fuel into the cylinders. Cams were probably first invented in ancient Greece.

A crankshaft, or crank, and its connecting rod work like an elbow joint. The crankshaft in a car engine converts the up and down motion of the pistons into rotary motion. They are also used to convert motion in the other way. One end of the crank is attached to the edge of a wheel. At the other end, the connecting rod cannot rotate, so it is pulled back and forth instead. Cranks were first used in ancient China around 100 c.e.

Alexandria described a gear-driven pulley system called a *barylkos* that could raise heavy weights with the turn of a handle.

ROTATIONAL ROMANS

The Greeks invented gears, but the Romans were the first people to make widespread use of them. Their wheel-based machines included simple grain mills turned around by donkeys, screw presses that crushed grapes for wine and olives for oil, and even a primitive combine harvester called a *vallus*. One of their best wheel-powered inventions was the treadmill, a bit like a giant mouse wheel turned around by slaves who trudged inside it. The engines of their day, treadmills were used to power a whole range of large machines, including water-raising devices, grain mills, olive presses, and even gigantic cranes.

Like the Greeks, the Romans also made use of water power. In 27 C.E., Roman architect Vitruvius (70–25 B.C.E.) suggested mounting waterwheels vertically, so they could be driven by the current much more efficiently. He built a mill driven by an undershot waterwheel, which had water running underneath it. Large wooden gear wheels transferred the power from the wheel to heavy stone mill wheels nearby. Overshot waterwheels, which have the water running over them, were invented in the fifth century, at the end of the Roman era.

POWER IN THE MIDDLE AGES

Despite its widespread use in sailing ships, wind power made little impact on land until the 12th century. Windmills had been invented in Persia (now Iran) about 600 years before, but they did not become common elsewhere for many centuries. One reason for this may have been the sheer number of water-powered mills that had already been constructed, especially in Europe. In England alone, for example, more than 5,600 water mills had been constructed by the sixth century. Once water mills had been built, there was no good reason to build windmills, except in dry places where powerful streams were rare.

The Middle Ages lasted roughly from the end of the Roman Empire to the 16th century. They are often seen as a low point in western civilization, when society, the arts, and technology developed at a very slow pace. Yet there were many advances to wheel power during this time. While the Greeks and Romans had relied on human and animal (*continued on page 27.*)

A hodometer was a Greek device that used wheels to measure distance. The machine was a modified cart. Crude gears linked the wheels to a drum. With each turn of the cart's wheel, the drum released a pebble into a bowl. At the end of the journey, counting the pebbles gave a measure of the distance traveled.

drum

cup

gear

cart

WORKING WHEELS

Windmills and water wheels are examples of *turbines*, devices that extract the energy from a moving fluid (liquid or gas) and use it to drive a machine.

Windmills do the job with large wooden sails. As they catch the wind, they slowly rotate a mighty central axle, known as the windshaft. Wheels and axles work in the same way as levers, so the bigger the sails on a windmill, the greater the torque (twisting force) at the

windshaft. Inside a windmill, gears of different shapes and sizes transfer power from the sails to the millstones. A huge vertical gear called the brake wheel rotates a horizontal one known as the wallower. That turns the great spur wheel, which in turn rotates the heavy millstones. The millstones crush grain into flour. Windmills work most efficiently when the sails face into the wind. Some windmills were built on a rotating base so they could

An undershot wheel in France is turned by a shallow river. Often rivers were diverted or narrowed to make them faster, so more energy was passed to the wheel.

be turned into the wind, no matter which way it was blowing. Some also had tail vanes that caught the wind and turned the sails to face the wind automatically.

Waterwheels extract power from rivers or seas using paddle wheels that turn as

kinetic energy of the moving water. Undershot wheels need the river to be always at the same level to work properly. Overshot waterwheels do not suffer from this problem and are typically up to eight times more efficient than undershot ones. They extract eight times more energy from the water.

Perhaps one of the largest water wheel systems ever built was constructed by the Romans at Barbégal, near Arles in the south of France around 300 C.E. Water from an aqueduct (a canal carried overhead on a bridge) was channeled down through a combination of sixteen large waterwheels, each driving a millstone 3 feet (0.9 m) across. This giant machine produced enough grain each day to feed all 12,500 people who lived in Arles.

the water passes by. The most familiar waterwheels stand upright and have a horizontal axle. Overshot waterwheels are turned around by water falling onto them from above. The energy they take from the water is a mixture of its potential energy, the energy it has because it is high up, and its kinetic energy, the energy the water has because it is moving. Undershot waterwheels have a river or stream flowing beneath them and are turned by just the

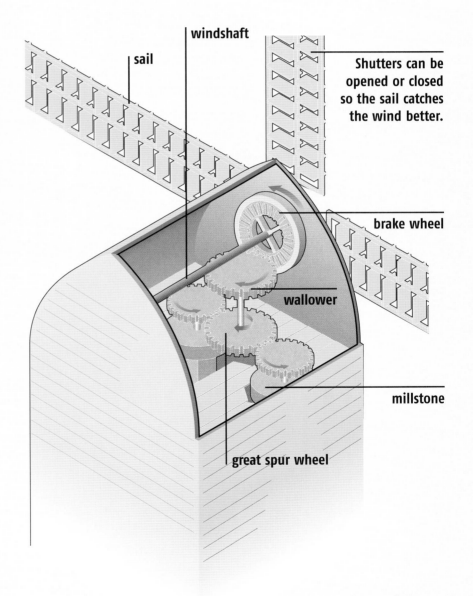

sail

windshaft

Shutters can be opened or closed so the sail catches the wind better.

brake wheel

wallower

millstone

great spur wheel

Windmill

Leonardo's Machines

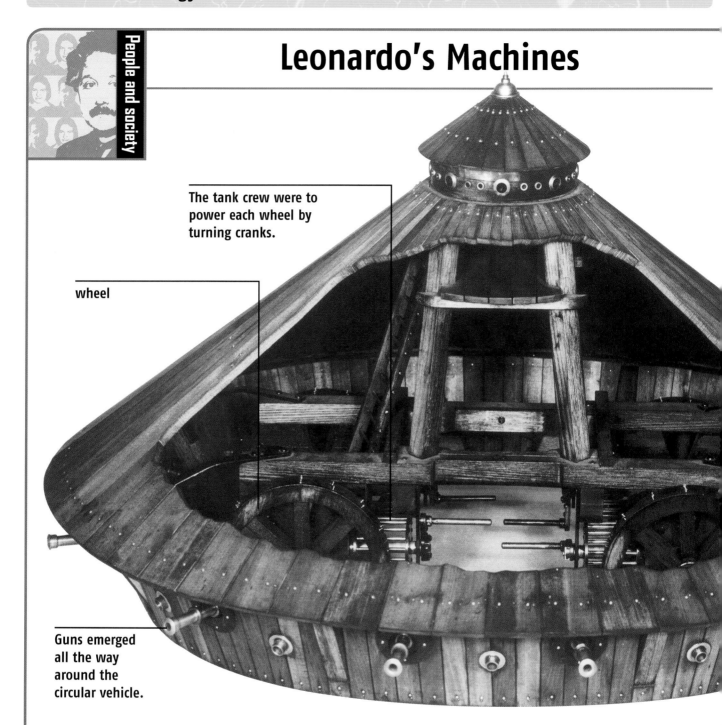

The tank crew were to power each wheel by turning cranks.

wheel

Guns emerged all the way around the circular vehicle.

Italian Renaissance artist Leonardo da Vinci (1452–1519) is best known for his beautiful paintings such as *Mona Lisa* and *The Last Supper*. However, as well as being the greatest artist of his age, da Vinci was also a great scientist and inventor. Although he did not build many of his ideas, and any that he did no longer survive, da Vinci left a record of his inventions in a huge number of sketches and plans. All da Vinci's designs were many years, if not centuries, ahead of their time. He made designs for several winged aircraft, a helicopter, and a parachute. He also thought up new technology for use on the battlefield, including an armored tank (model above) and machine gun.

Although da Vinci's designs show he had an incredible imagination, none of them would have worked. The artist did not understand forces and energy, so his machines were too heavy to move with the power sources available.

Wooden shell sloped to deflect cannonballs.

power, by the end of the Middle Ages, windmills and water wheels were the major sources of power. The wheel also brought many other advances. Carts made it much easier for people to travel and transport their goods. Plows fitted with wheels were better at digging fields for planting, making farming more productive. Spinning wheels also made it easier to produce the threads used in textiles. People used the wheels to make their own clothes.

It was impossible to make early wooden wheels in exact sizes for precision wheels. The invention of precise metal gears, however, made many new devices possible, such as accurate clocks.

A history enthusiast uses a pole lathe, a simple machine that used rotary motion to shape wood. He is spinning a piece of wood with a cord attached to a pedal.

PRECISION GEARS

Gears not only made large and powerful machines, such as cranes and mills, possible, but they were also an essential part in the development of high-precision machines, such as clocks, chronometers, and even the first computers.

HOW CLOCKS WORK
A clock is essentially a machine that uses regular movement to mark different periods of time. In a pendulum clock, the back-and-forth swinging of a heavy metal weight, the pendulum, turns the gears that, in turn, move the hands around. In a pocket watch, a tiny spring, called a hairspring, moves back and forth and takes the place of the pendulum. In a digital watch, the regular movement comes from tiny electric pulses from a quartz crystal driven by a battery.

Wristwatch

1. The tiny hairspring moves back and forth creating the rhythm that drives the watch.

2. The escape wheel is attached to the spring by an arm, called an anchor. The wheel turns with every movement of the spring.

3. The movement of the escape wheel is passed through other gear wheels to the center wheel, which connects to the watch's hands.

4. A coil inside the barrel wheel is wound up each day. The tension in this coil pulls on the hairspring, connected through the gears, and keeps the watch running.

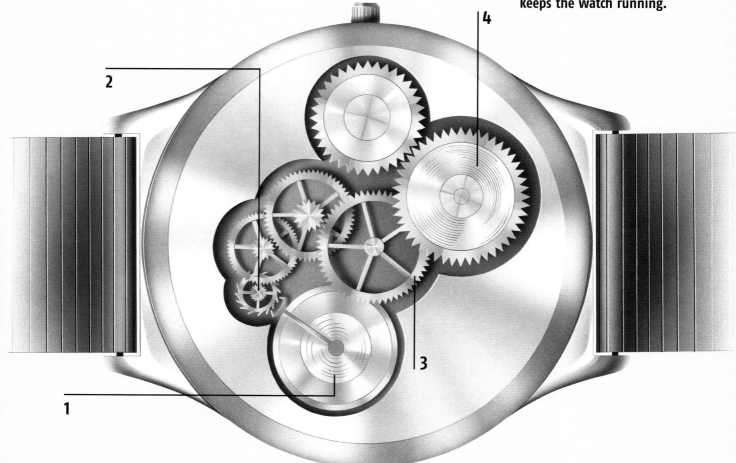

Unlike in a large machine, where the gears are designed to increase power, the job of a clock's gears is to make the hands move around at different speeds. The hour, minute, and second hands are all driven by the movement of a single wheel, but gears ensure that the second hand moves around the clockface exactly 60 times faster than the minute hand, which moves 12 times faster than the hour hand.

CLOCK HISTORY

Historians believe the Chinese invented the first mechanical clock in the 11th century. Early clocks were very large. One made for the French king by Henry De Vick in the 14th century was driven by a 500-pound (227-kg) weight that rose and fell through a height of 32 feet (9.8 m). Pendulums and balance springs were invented in the early 17th century. These innovations made clocks more accurate and more compact. High-precision clocks were developed in the 18th century. English clockmaker John Harrison (1693–1776), showed that accurate clocks could be used aboard ships to calculate longitude, the position east or west.

FROM CLOCKS TO COMPUTERS

The precision gears that told the time found their way into other machines as well. The 17th century brought accurate scientific instruments, such as *orreries*—small gear-driven models of the planets. Early calculators and computers also used gear wheels. Devised by French scientist Blaise Pascal (1623–62) in 1642, the first calculator of

The world's first calculator invented by mathematician Blaise Pascal. It used gears to calculate the answer to additions that were inputed by turning dials on the front.

this sort used ten gear wheels to add and subtract. A more powerful calculator produced by German inventor and philosopher Gottfried Leibniz (1646–1716) used gear wheels to multiply numbers as well.

In the 19th century, English inventor Charles Babbage (1792–1871) made what is generally considered to be the very first computer using many hundreds of high-precision gear wheels. But his plans for bigger and better computers were defeated because it was too difficult and costly to make gear wheels that were precise enough for his purposes.

POWERING THE REVOLUTION

James Watt, the steam engineer, contemplates some improvements to his engine as he watches water boiling on a fire.

Although wind and water power were a huge advance on muscle power, they were not without their drawbacks. Windmills could operate only on windy days, while waterwheels had to be built near rivers. However, steam engines, which were developed in the 18th century, could be used almost anywhere, making power available whenever it was needed. This advance laid the foundations for the Industrial Revolution in the early 19th century.

EARLY DAYS OF STEAM

The first person to generate power with steam was probably ancient Greek inventor Hero of Alexandria in the first century. The idea was largely forgotten again until the late Middle Ages, but it was revived in the 16th century by Italian architect Giovanni Branca (1571–1640). He developed a simple steam turbine in which a continuous flow of steam pushed around a wheel fitted with paddles.

More advances took place during the 17th century, when scientists began to understand gases properly for the first time. In 1660, British chemist Robert Boyle (1627–91) worked out a series of laws to explain how gases behave at different temperatures and pressures. One of his most important findings was that the pressure of a gas increases if it is heated in a closed container. If the gas is then allowed to expand, it can drive a machine.

The first engine—an energy-producing machine—to use this idea was designed in 1680 by Dutch physicist Christiaan Huygens (1629–95). His design had a large upright cylinder with a piston

inside it. Huygens found he could make the piston rise and fall by exploding small charges of gunpowder inside the cylinder. Relying on gunpowder was not the most practical way of making energy, however. Huygens had a French assistant named Denis Papin (1647–1712) who had worked with Robert Boyle. Using his knowledge of gases, Papin

The Science of Pressure

How things work

Gas hits container walls, exerting pressure.

More gas in the same space exerts higher pressure.

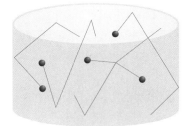

Colder gas moves more slowly and exerts lower pressure.

Many different machines, from tiny tools such as drawing pins to mighty locomotives pushed forward by the power of steam, rely on pressure to work. Pressure is the amount of force that acts over an area. When you push on a drawing pin, you put a certain amount of force on the large flat head. But the same amount of force travels down the pin itself to the sharp, narrow point. The same force acts on both the large head of the pin and the narrow point. But the area of the point is much less than the area of the head, so the pressure is greater at the point and the pin penetrates the wall. Pressure is defined as the size of the force that pushes divided by the area over which it acts.

Gases, such as steam or oxygen, exert a certain pressure because of the way molecules move around inside them. In an oxygen cylinder, gas molecules move around chaotically, crashing into

one another and into the cylinder walls. Each time they collide with the walls, they push against them. Millions of molecules making millions of collisions with the walls exert a very large force—and a very high pressure. When a gas gets hotter, the molecules move more quickly and collide more often. It is this phenomenon that makes hotter gases exert a greater pressure than cooler ones. Squeezing the same amount of gas into a smaller space also increases its pressure because there are more collisions with the smaller container walls.

Pressure is the key to how steam engines work. When steam enters the cylinder, the piston moves outward. This happens because the pressure of the hot steam on the inside of the piston is greater than the pressure of the cold air on the outside. The hotter the steam, the more energy it contains, and the greater the power the engine produces.

came up with a better design in which the piston was driven by steam. At the time, coal was fast becoming the most popular fuel, and many mines were being dug to meet the demand. Flooding was a major problem in the mines. In in 1698, English engineer Thomas Savery designed a steam engine to pump water out of the deep shafts. His coal-fueled machine is regarded as the world's first practical steam engine.

ENGINES IN PRACTICE

A steam engine works by first turning water into steam and then allowing this gas to expand in a confined space. As it expands, it pushes against a piston and turns heat energy into motion. Early engines were impractical because they tried to perform the two phases in the same part of the machine. The innovation that led to the first practical steam engines was to generate the steam in a boiler. The steam then expanded inside a cylinder, which was fitted with a movable piston.

The first person to build an engine like this was English blacksmith Thomas Newcomen (1663–1729), who improved Thomas Savery's earlier engine. In Newcomen's engine, the piston was inside an upright cylinder. As the steam expanded in the cylinder, it pushed the piston up. The cylinder was then cooled down with liquid water. The cooler steam took up less space, and the piston fell back down. The up-and

-down motion of the piston moved a long mechanical arm that was used to pump water out of mines.

Newcomen's engines were a great success and more than 1,000 were built. But they were slow and inefficient because the cylinder had to be first heated up

A diagram of one of Thomas Newcomen's steam engines. The huge machine moved a pivoted arm that pumped water.

to make the piston rise and then cooled down to make the piston fall. A Scottish instrument maker named James Watt (1736–1819) studied Newcomen's engine and made several improvements. The biggest change he made was to add a condenser, where the steam could be cooled down. This freed up the cylinder to be filled with fresh high-pressure steam. Watt also used cranks to turn the piston's up-and-down motion into rotational motion that could drive a wheel. Watt's innovations made him a very rich man, while Newcomen hardly profited at all.

THE AGE OF STEAM

Watt's riches were well deserved because his engines were the most powerful machines ever made. His innovations made steam engines efficient enough to be widely used, and they were soon powering the world's first factories

People and society

The First Steam Engine?

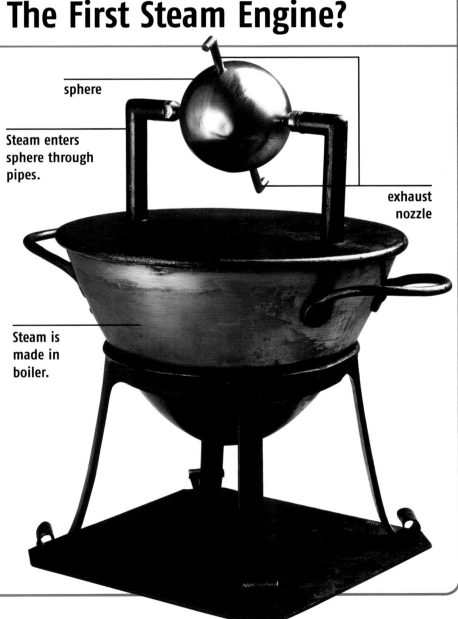

sphere

Steam enters sphere through pipes.

exhaust nozzle

Steam is made in boiler.

Most people think steam engines were invented by Thomas Newcomen and James Watt. In fact, the very first steam engine was developed by Greek inventor Hero of Alexandria, who lived in Egypt in the first century. Hero's engine, which he called an *aeolipile* (model, right), was a hollow sphere that had two exhaust nozzles on opposite sides and pointing in opposite directions. Hero filled the ball with water and placed it over a fire. As the water boiled, steam gushed from the two nozzles and made the ball spin around. Although Hero's steam engine could not power other machines, it was a good demonstration of how heat energy in the steam could be converted into mechanical energy, which made the ball rotate.

as the Industrial Revolution began. But even Watt's engines still suffered from a major drawback: They were large, cumbersome, and fixed in one place. The reason they were so big was that they used steam at low pressures, roughly the same pressure as the air in the atmosphere. This meant there had to be a great deal of steam pushing a very large piston to do any useful work.

The answer seemed to be to develop smaller engines that used higher pressure steam. In Britain, it was mining engineer Richard Trevithick (1771–1833) who first developed machines of this kind.

How things work

How Steam Engines Work

A steam engine converts the heat energy in steam into more useful mechanical motion that can drive a variety of machines. When hot steam is allowed to expand, it cools down and gives up its energy. A steam engine works by taking in a certain amount of steam, allowing it to expand and then cool as its energy is converted into mechanical work. The process is repeated many times.

The two key components of a steam engine are a boiler, where the steam is produced, and a cylinder, where the steam is allowed to expand. The cylinder is a hollow metal can with a piston inside. The piston is free to move up and down the cylinder.

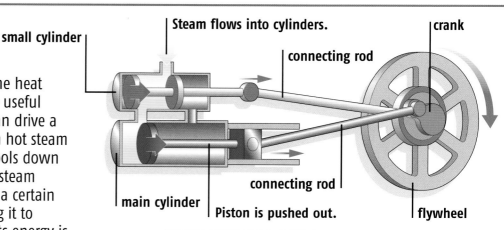

small cylinder | **Steam flows into cylinders.** | **crank**
connecting rod
main cylinder | **connecting rod**
Piston is pushed out. | **flywheel**

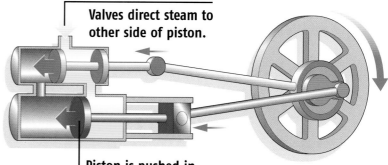

Valves direct steam to other side of piston.

Piston is pushed in.

A steam engine produces its motion in two phases. At first, the boiler feeds steam into the cylinder through an opening called an inlet valve. As the steam expands, it pushes the piston up the cylinder. The piston is connected to a large flywheel by a two-piece mechanism called a crank, which is attached to the wheel, and a connecting rod, attached to the piston. As the piston moves out, it turns the flywheel. The flywheel is so heavy that it keeps on spinning even when the piston reaches the end of the cylinder. As the wheel keeps on moving, it begins to push the piston in the opposite direction. In earlier steam engines, the flywheel's motion could only push the piston back to its original position, flushing the cooled steam from the cylinder. Later, more efficient engines used steam to both pull and push the piston in and out (as above). Valves controlled the flow of steam into and out of the the cylinder. Some engines increased their power by using the steam to power two or more pistons.

Key inventions

Coke: The Cleaner Coal

Coke is a high-energy, smokeless fuel made by heating coal to remove the impurities. The fuel is hard and dark gray and is made up of about 90 percent carbon. The remaining 10 percent is ash containing nitrogen, sulfur, and other chemicals. Although a coke-making process was devised in England in 1622, it was almost a century before the fuel was used in large quantities. In 1709, English industrialist Abraham Darby (1677–1717) discovered that it was cheaper to use coke instead of charcoal for making iron. Inexpensive iron made it easier to build steam engines and other machines (in a forge, above). Coke and iron were the materials that made the Industrial Revolution possible.

In the United States, similar engines were produced by a miller named Oliver Evans (1755–1819). These engines worked at very much higher pressures (14 times atmospheric pressure), so they could do much more work than earlier engines and be smaller, too. Thanks to Trevithick and Evans, high-pressure engines were soon small enough to power vehicles. Evans developed a steam road carriage in 1789 and also designed small but powerful engines to run textile mills and other factories. Trevithick devoted his attention to making steam-powered rail locomotives.

THE MINER'S FRIEND

Fire and water have always been regarded as powerful elements, so there was great excitement in 1698 when English army officer Captain Thomas Savery (1650–1715) patented his Engine to Raise Water by Fire. Better known as the Miner's Friend, because it pumped out water from flooded mines, Savery's invention was the world's first practical steam engine.

Savery was from Cornwall, which is the southwest corner of England famous for its many metal and coal mines and stone quarries. Flooding has always been a problem for miners, and it was getting worse as the high demand for coal and other useful minerals drove miners to dig deeper than ever before.

The problem of how to empty water from deep mine shafts soon captured Savery's attention. Having studied the work of Denis Papin and Christiaan Huygens in France, he thought he could develop a steam engine similar to their's that would pump out the waste water automatically.

Nothing like Savery's engine had been seen before, and it caused quite a stir. But it suffered a major drawback.

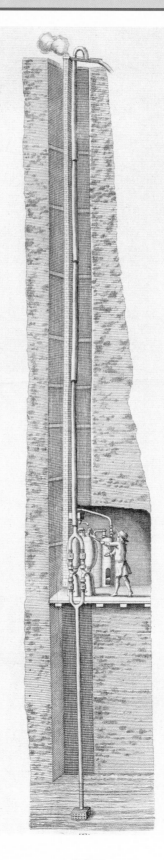

It used low-pressure steam, so it was not very powerful. It struggled to raise water much higher than about 20 feet (6 m) so it was useless in the deeper mines. Savery tried and failed to make higher pressure engines. At the time, people did not know how to make iron strong enough to construct boilers and pipes that could withstand high-pressure steam.

In his patent, Savery suggested the Miner's Friend could be used in "...all sorts of mills, where they have not the benefit of water nor constant winds." Although it is hard to see how his machine could do this, Savery must have glimpsed a future where steam engines would one day replace waterwheels and windmills as a more practical source of power. Although barely remembered today, Savery was a true visionary who could see that steam engines such as the Miner's Friend would soon change the world.

A diagram showing how a Miner's Friend could be installed into a mine shaft that suffered from flooding.

How the Miner's Friend Worked

Savery's machine did not use pistons and cylinders like the steam engines that followed it. It had no moving parts at all, but made use of the relationship between the pressure and temperature of a gas to exert forces on flood water.

The engine's main components were two large water-filled vessels. Each vessel could be attached to a boiler that made steam and a cooling cold-water reservoir. Each vessel worked alternately: As one was sucking water up from the mine, the other was squirting water out the top of the shaft. Each vessel followed four steps:

1. The vessel on the right contains water that has already been drawn up from the mine. Hot steam from the boiler is directed into this vessel through the open faucet at the top.

2. The steam is at a higher pressure than the atmosphere. It therefore pushes down on the water, forcing it out of the vessel, up the machine's tube, and out of the mine. A valve in the base of the vessel is kept closed to stop water flowing back down the mine.

3. When all the water has been forced out, and the vessel is full of hot high-pressure steam, the boiler is disconnected and the faucet at the top is closed.

4. Cold water from a reservoir is now sprayed on the side of the vessel. This cools the steam inside and reduces its pressure to below that of the atmosphere. The valve at the bottom of the vessel is now opened. The gases in the atmosphere, which are pushing down on the water in the mine, force it up into the vessel. Once the vessel is full of water, the process is repeated.

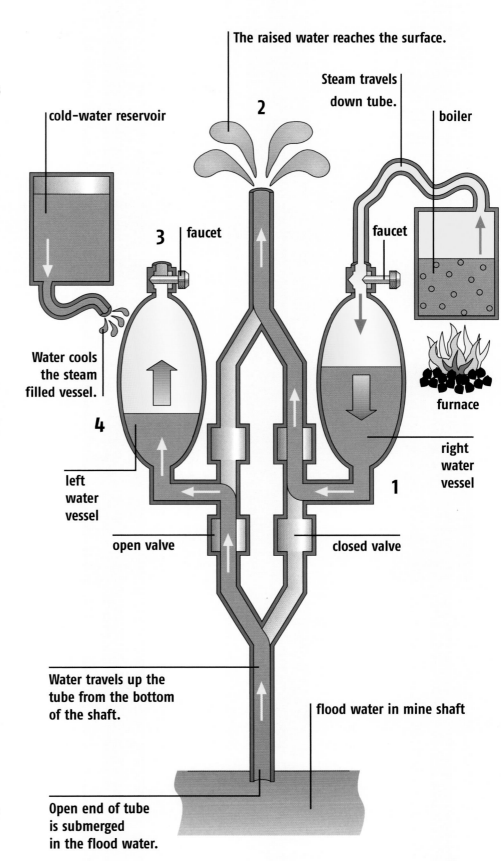

The raised water reaches the surface.

Steam travels down tube.

2

cold-water reservoir

boiler

3 | faucet

faucet

Water cools the steam filled vessel.

4

furnace

left water vessel

right water vessel

1

open valve

closed valve

Water travels up the tube from the bottom of the shaft.

flood water in mine shaft

Open end of tube is submerged in the flood water.

FOSSIL FUELS

The Roman Empire ran on slaves. With so many slaves available, engines driven by people, such as treadmills, were the best source of power. In much the same way, it was the abundant supply of coal and other fossil fuels that enabled steam engines to power the mines, factories, and locomotives of the 19th-century Industrial Revolution. Fossil fuels have been people's biggest source of energy ever since, but their widespread use has led to serious environmental problems, such as air pollution and changes to Earth's climate.

HOW FOSSIL FUELS ARE MADE
Fuels such as coal and petroleum occur naturally in Earth's crust, but they were not always present in the rocks deep underground. As their name suggests, fossil fuels are made when plants and animals die and eventually form fossils. Peat, a crumbly organic material

An off-shore drilling platform extracts crude oil from deep beneath the seabed. The oil comes to the surface mixed with mud and sand and also contains natural gas. It is too expensive to collect the gas, which is burned off in a huge flame.

Combustion

Combustion is the process by which a fuel burns in oxygen gas to give off heat. The chemical reaction that takes place looks like this:

Hydrocarbon fuel + oxygen gas
=
carbon dioxide gas + water

The fuel is made from carbon and hydrogen atoms. During combustion, the chemical bonds that hold the atoms together are broken apart. New bonds are then formed between carbon and oxygen (making carbon dioxide) and between hydrogen and oxygen (making water).

While it takes energy to break chemical bonds, more energy is released as the new bonds are formed. Chemical bonds store a type of potential energy, so breaking them can give off energy. Some of this energy is used to form the chemical bonds that turn the fuel and oxygen into carbon dioxide and water. But there is a great deal of energy left over, and this is why combustion gives off so much heat.

Other reactions can also take place during combustion. If there is not enough oxygen to burn the fuel completely, poisonous carbon monoxide gas is also produced. This is one of the reasons why household fires and stoves always need a good supply of ventilation. If there are impurities such as sulfur in the fuel, foul-smelling sulfur dioxide gas is produced as a byproduct as well.

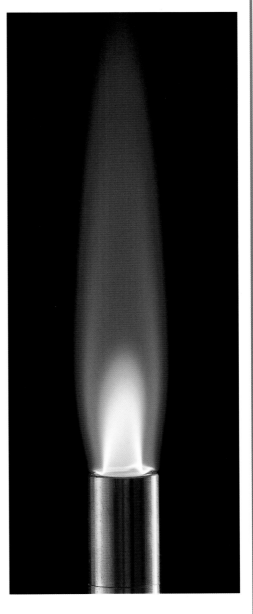

Carbon monoxide and sulfur dioxide are two of the dangerous gases that cause air pollution.

When solid or liquid fuel gets hot, it turns into gas. It is the gas that burns, and the heat and light it releases forms a flickering flame. The color of a flame is an indication of how hot it is. Blue flames, like burning gas (above), are the hottest, while red ones are the coolest.

Under-Floor Heating

Central heating is one of the luxuries of modern living, but it was invented during Roman times, more than 2,000 years ago. The Romans designed their buildings with air spaces under the floors (above, in Pompeii, Italy) and ducts running between the walls. Hot air and smoke from a furnace were channeled into the floor and wall spaces. The heat from one furnace was enough to warm the whole building, so fires did not have to be kept in every room. The Romans called their central heating systems *hypocausts*—a Greek word meaning "fire underneath."

found in bogs and swamps, is formed when wetland plants decay. As layers of other materials, such as sand and mud, build up on top, the peat gets squashed down. Over about 300 million years, the compressed peat turns into layers of coal. Petroleum is produced in a similar way, but forms from the remains of tiny sea algae and animals called plankton. Being compressed by thick layers of rock causes a huge rise in temperature and pressure and, after millions of

Oil Platforms

One third of oil and gas comes from under the seabed. Offshore drilling rigs are used to extract it.

1. Oil and gas rises up through porous rock.

2. Non-porous cap rock creates a reservoir.

3. Gas reservoir floats on top of the trapped oil.

4. Well heads on the seafloor connect to tankers on the surface.

5. Some large oil platforms stand on the seabed and have many well heads.

6. A heavy concrete tank stores oil and keeps the platform stable.

7. Oil is pumped to the shore through a pipeline.

years, deposits of oil and gas become trapped in reservoirs of rock and sand. Some of the world's coal and petroleum deposits have been thrust back to the surface as the crust buckles and breaks. Most of the largest supplies are deep underground, and have to be removed by mining or drilling.

TYPES OF FOSSIL FUELS

Petroleum is the most widely used fossil fuel today, largely because is used to make gasoline and other fuel for cars, aircraft, and some ships. Most petroleum forms under the sea and occurs in both liquid and gas forms. Crude (unrefined) oil is rich in a range of hydrocarbons. Hydrocarbons are chemicals made of hydrogen and carbon, and the most useful ones are separated out, or refined.

Petroleum has been extracted from the ground in large quantities since the middle of the 19th century. Since that time, people have removed and consumed more than half of Earth's total reserves. Estimates vary over how long the planet's remaining supplies will last. In 1874, Pennsylvania's state geologists (rock scientists) warned that oil would run out within just four years. Advances in technology for finding and drilling for oil have enabled geologists to push back their estimates many times since then. Whether oil ever will run out or simply become too expensive to extract remains unknown. Geologists believe oil production will begin a long, but steady decline during the early decades of the 21st century. But problems with the environment, such as

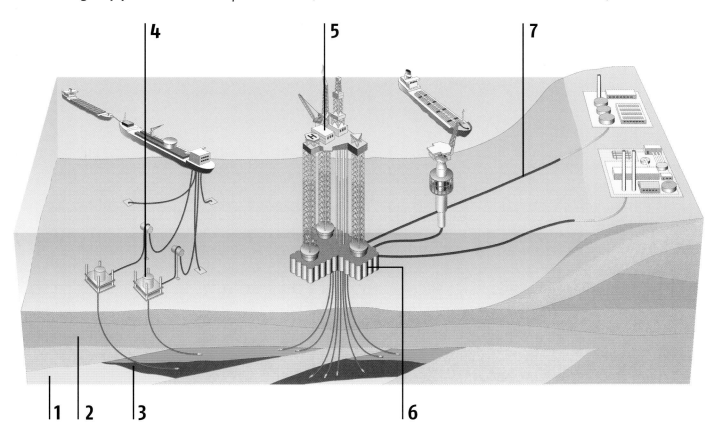

How things work

Useful Chemicals

A chemical compound made from hydrogen and carbon is called a hydrocarbon. Hydrogen and carbon can be combined in any number of ways, and fossil fuels such as petroleum typically contain a mixture of many different hydrocarbons. When crude oil (above) is processed in an oil refinery, its hydrocarbon components are separated out. These include gasoline, kerosene (aircraft fuel), asphalt, lubricant oils, gas oil, and a number of other compounds. Once they have been extracted, these hydrocarbons are used to make a range of products, from paints and plastics to fuels

global warming and pollution, may cause people to switch to alternative power sources before the Earth's oil runs out completely.

It was the invention of the gasoline and diesel engines, toward the end of the 19th century that led to such widespread use of petroleum. Before that time, steam engines had turned coal into the world's favorite fuel. Unlike petroleum, coal is a solid fuel. Different types of coal contain varying amounts of carbon. Peat, from which coal is originally formed, is high in moisture and contains the least carbon. Coke, a type of coal that has been heated in air to remove impurities, is about 90 percent carbon. Graphite and diamond are almost completely pure carbon.

An excavator moves a huge pile of coal. Coal is either found deep underground or close to the surface. Surface mines like this one strip away the topsoil to get at the coal beneath. Deeper mines extract coal through long shafts.

Coal is used much less widely today than during the Industrial Revolution. This is partly because it is such a dirty fuel and partly because oil and gas can be used more efficiently. Even as recently as the 1920s, coal supplied about three-quarters of all the energy people used. Today, only a quarter of our energy comes from coal. Some industrializing nations, such as China, continue to burn large amounts of coal in power plants and in factories. They suffer very bad air pollution as a result.

China uses so much coal because it still has huge reserves. The world as a whole is estimated to have several hundred years of coal supplies left to be mined.

Petroleum and coal are often used, not in their familiar liquid and solid forms, but as gases. Petroleum occurs naturally as a gas in very deep underground deposits. Coal can be turned into coal gas (a mixture of carbon monoxide and methane) easily. Petroleum gas (pure methane) is supplied to homes and industry by

Crude oil goes through many processes as it is refined. These include cooling and heating the oil to separate different "fractions," or groups of chemicals. Less useful chemicals are also "cracked," or broken apart into much more useful substances.

Keeping Warm

Temperatures on Earth can vary dramatically from one season to the next, and keeping warm has always been one of our biggest problems. The simplest heating system is an open fire (above). The first fuels used by people included wood, dung, and turf. Charcoal is wood that has been heated to burn away impurities. This proved to be a better fuel than ordinary firewood because it produced much less smoke. During the Industrial Revolution, wood was replaced by coal, which produced much more heat. Coal itself gave way to smokeless coke, used in iron and steel production.

It was not just the fuels that evolved, ways of burning them improved, too. Chimneys were invented in the 13th century as a way of keeping the smoke out of a building and improving the airflow through a fire. In the 17th century, basic fires were enclosed in metal grates that stood off the ground. These were safer for holding coal than open fires and also increased the air flowing through them. Electricity and central heating have made fires obsolete in modern homes. They are, however, the only ways of heating and cooking for many people living in developing nations.

pipelines or in large tanks. It is burned directly in boilers, stoves, and gas fires. This so-called natural gas is inexpensive and cleaner than coal and oil, and it produces a lot of heat when burned. Because of this it has become one of the most popular fossil fuels used in modern power plants. When gases are stored under pressure, they turn into liquids and take up less room. Liquid petroleum gas (LPG), as this is known, can be used to power cars instead of gasoline. A similar technique is used to make liquid fuel for camping stoves and cigarette lighters.

GLOBAL WARMING

If scientists are right, Earth is getting warmer, the seas are rising, and there could be dramatic changes in climate during the not too distant future. These changes are part of a phenomenon called global warming, which is thought to be caused by people burning fossil fuels.

Global warming is driven by the greenhouse effect, so called because the Earth warms up in a similar way to a greenhouse. Light and heat from the Sun enters Earth's atmosphere and warms the planet. The warmed Earth gives off some of this heat.

However, gases, such as carbon dioxide and methane, in the atmosphere act like the glass in a greenhouse and stop some of the heat from escaping. This makes Earth much warmer than it would otherwise be.

The greenhouse effect is a natural process. Without it Earth would be too cold for life to survive. By burning fuels, however, people have upset the balance of the gases in the air. When fuels are burned, the process produces carbon dioxide and other greenhouse gases. Since the Industrial Revolution, 200

Ice crashes into the sea as a thick ice sheet in Antarctica melts. Global warming may make sea levels rise, as more polar ice melts and seawater expands.

years ago, the amount of greenhouse gas in Earth's atmosphere has increased by about a third. In other words, the "glass" in Earth's "greenhouse" has become "thicker," and the planet is now warming up as a result.

Some scientists think the changes to the weather will be dramatic, since Earth may now have more carbon dioxide in its atmosphere than at any time during the last 20 million years of history.

It is very difficult to work out what the results of global warming will be. While the Earth as a whole will probably warm up, some regions may experience colder weather and extreme storms.

The planet could heat up by anything from 2 to 7 degrees by the end of this century. This does not sound like much and, at first sight, a warmer Earth might appear to be a good thing. Winters would be shorter, days would be warmer, and crops might grow better. In fact, Earth's climate is much more finely balanced than this. As the warmer seawater expands, sea levels could rise by almost 3 feet (0.9 m), which could make tens of millions of people homeless in low-lying coastal areas. Weather will become more extreme, as the difference between hotter and cooler regions increases. Plants and animals that have adapted to living in particular regions may no longer be able to survive as their environment changes.

Although some scientists dispute whether the climate is really changing, most of the world's scientists now agree that global warming is a huge long-term threat to future generations.

Global Warming

The greenhouse effect is a natural atmospheric process. However, by adding gases, people may have begun to alter the climate.

1. Heat and light arrives from the Sun. Some is reflected into space, while the rest warms Earth.

2. Some of Earth's heat travels out of the atmosphere into space.

3. Some of the Earth's heat is trapped inside the atmosphere by the greenhouse gases.

4. Power plants release gases carbon dioxide and water vapor into the atmosphere by burning fuels.

5. Trees and other plants absorb carbon dioxide from the air. As forests are cut down, there are less trees available to do this.

6. Chemicals once used in aerosol cans and refrigerators are also greenhouse gases.

7. Greenhouse gases released by cars burning gasoline and diesel fuel.

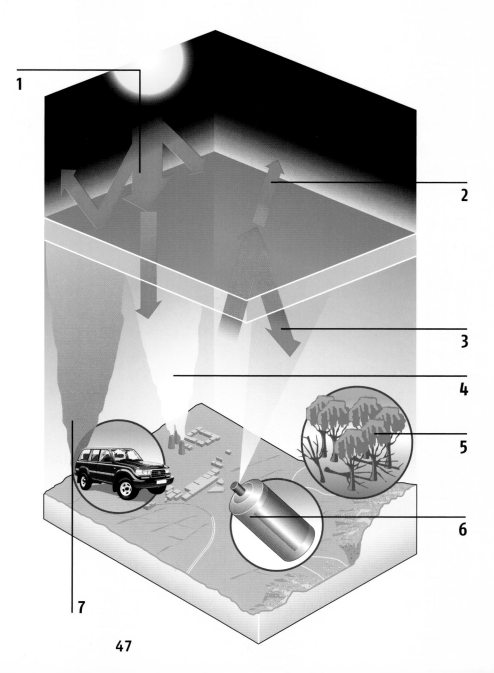

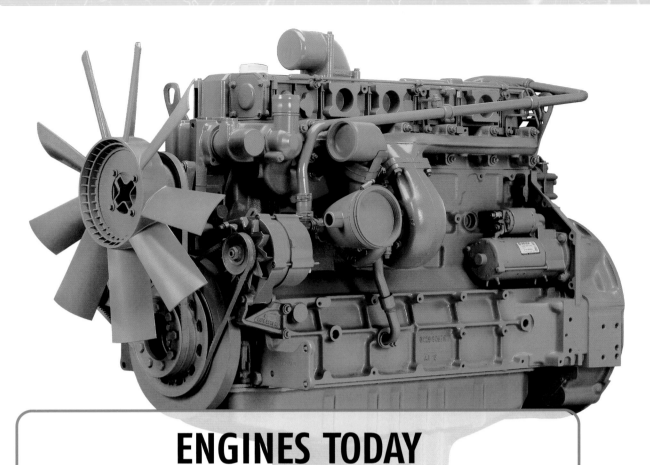

ENGINES TODAY

Even the best steam engines were not very efficient. During the late 19th century, engineers developed several new types of engine that were smaller, more practical and efficient than steam power. Many of these engines are still in widespread use today.

INTERNAL COMBUSTION

Several advances in design and metalworking made steam engines a lot more efficient over the years. In 1824, however, a French military engineer named Nicolas Sadi Carnot (1796–1832) figured out that there was a definite limit to how much they could be improved. The pioneers of steam,

such as Savery, Newcomen, and Watt, had developed inventions by trial and error. But Carnot used math to prove that steam-powered engines could only be about 30 percent efficient. In other words, even the best steam engine wasted at least two thirds of the coal it burned!

One of the main problems with a steam engine was that the place where steam was produced was separate from the place where heat energy was converted into mechanical energy. A lot of energy was lost as hot steam traveled from the boiler to the cylinder. This system is known as external combustion because the fuel is

Unlike steam engines, internal-combustion engines can be a wide range of sizes for use in many machines. For example, the huge diesel engine above is used to power mobile cranes and excavators. It works in the same way, however, as the smaller gasoline engine that drives a hand-held chain saw.

combusted, or burned, outside the cylinder. Other inventors thought they could produce better engines that burned fuel inside the cylinder. This is system is called internal combustion.

When Dutch physicist Christiaan Huygens (1629–95) exploded gunpowder in the cylinder of an engine, he invented the idea of internal combustion. His invention, although completely

Key inventions

Steam Turbine

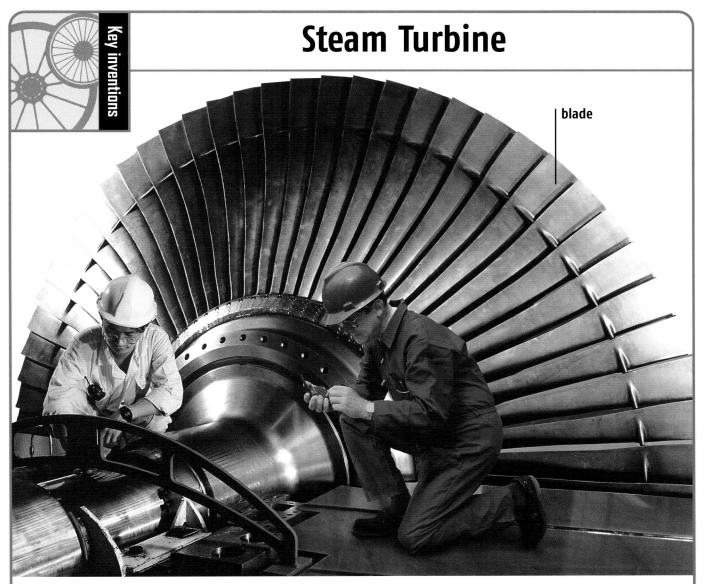

blade

British engineer Sir Charles Parsons (1854–1931) changed ship engines and electricity generators for ever in 1884 when he invented the steam turbine. During the early 20th century, steam turbines were widely used to power warships and ocean liners. They are still used to generate electricity in most power plants today. Unlike a traditional steam engine, which makes its power with pistons and cylinders, a steam turbine produces power when

steam flows through a turbine—thin blades arranged in a spinning wheel (above). Turbines work like the sails of a windmill, only they are made from metal and turn around at very high speeds. Steam turbines generally have several sets of wheels known as stages. Each one extracts power from the steam rushing past it. As the stages spin, they turn an axle. This drives a machine directly or can be used to power an electricity generator.

Key inventions

Stirling Engine

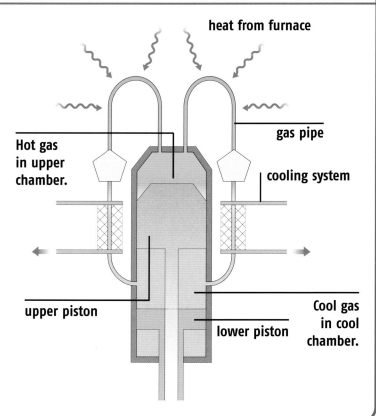

In 1816, a Scottish minister named Robert Stirling (1790–1878) invented a new type of external combustion engine. Inside a Stirling engine, a fixed amount of gas, generally hydrogen or helium, is cooled inside a chamber. As the pressure in the chamber drops, a lower piston rises up toward an upper piston. This pushes the gas through pipes into an upper chamber. On the way, the gas is heated by a furnace and expands as it enters the second chamber. The hot gas pushes both pistons down. The upper piston then begins to rise, creating a low-pressure space beneath it. Gas drawn from the hot chamber into the lower space is cooled on the way, and the cycle begins over. Stirling's engine is one of the most fuel-efficient ever invented, a third more efficient than an internal-combustion engine.

impractical, eventually led to the steam engine. The first person to build a practical internal-combustion engine was Belgian-born French engineer Jean Joseph Étienne Lenoir (1822–1900). In 1860, he converted a steam engine so that its cylinders burned coal gas. Coal gas is a fuel made by heating coal. It is mainly carbon monoxide gas and was used to power street lamps at the time. By 1865, nearly 1,500 of Lenoir's engines were in use. Most of them powered industrial machines, such as printing presses, but Lenoir managed to drive both a simple automobile and a small boat with later versions of his engine.

GASOLINE ENGINES

In 1862, another French engineer named Alphonse Beau de Rochas (1815–93) designed a better internal-combustion engine. His engine repeated four processes. Firstly, a mixture of fuel and air is drawn into the cylinder as the piston falls. It is then compressed as the piston rises. Next the fuel is ignited, and the explosion drives the piston down. The piston rises again, flushing the exhaust gas from the cylinder, making it ready again for the first phase. This so-called four-stroke cycle is repeated many times. The up-and-down motion of the piston is converted to rotary motion by a crank.

Diesel Engine

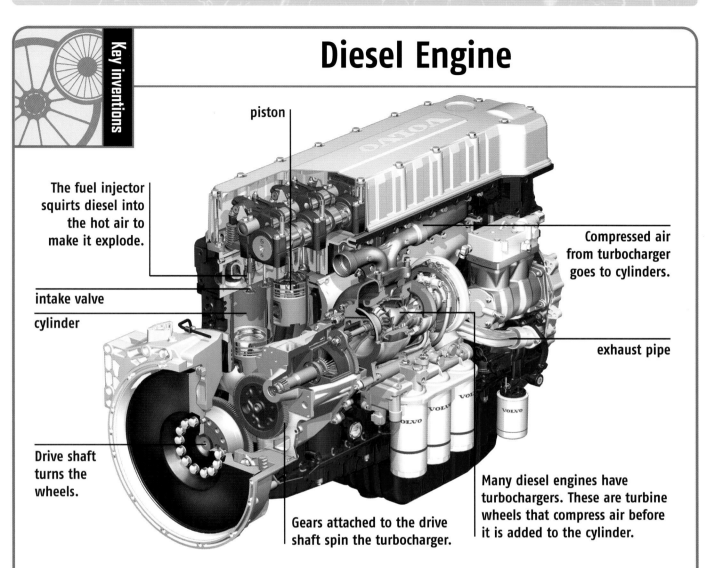

piston

The fuel injector squirts diesel into the hot air to make it explode.

intake valve

cylinder

Compressed air from turbocharger goes to cylinders.

exhaust pipe

Drive shaft turns the wheels.

Gears attached to the drive shaft spin the turbocharger.

Many diesel engines have turbochargers. These are turbine wheels that compress air before it is added to the cylinder.

In 1885, German engineer, Rudolf Diesel (1858–1913) devised an internal-combustion engine that did not run on gasoline. It used a heavier oil (now called diesel) as its fuel instead.

A diesel engine (above) works a lot like a gasoline engine, but with one big difference. In a gasoline engine, a spark plug ignites the mixture of fuel and air inside the cylinder. In a diesel engine, the fuel–air mixture is compressed much more, so it occupies about 20 times less space. Squeezing the mixture this much makes it so hot that it ignites all by itself and burns much more efficiently. One drawback of this is that diesel engines have to be heavier and sturdier to operate at higher pressures. This is why they are typically used in large vehicles, such as trucks and railroad locomotives. Diesel engines are generally more efficient than gasoline-powered ones and also use less expensive fuel.

Rochas never built his engine, but in 1867, German Nikolaus August Otto (1832–91) built a gasoline-powered version. This proved to be a real alternative to steam power. The design was improved yet again a few years later by Gottlieb Daimler (1834 –1900). He used it to power his early cars. Daimler added an extra chamber above the cylinder, known as a carburetor, where the fuel and air could be properly mixed so they burned more efficiently.

GAS TURBINES

The energy produced by an engine comes from the fuel it burns. A very efficient type of internal-combustion engine can produce much more energy from the same amount of fuel as an inefficient steam engine. Engines with more cylinders burn more fuel and produce more power. But there is still a limit to how much power can be produced by ordinary internal-combustion engines, even if it has many cylinders.

Large machines, such as ships and airplanes, need a larger and better type of internal-combustion engine called a gas turbine. Gas turbines, or jet engines, are very unlike the engines used in cars. They are large metal cylinders that have a fan at the front end, a combustion chamber in the middle, and an exhaust nozzle at the back end.

The fan sucks in air. The air is compressed by a series of smaller fans. This makes the air hot. The hot air is mixed with fuel in the combustion chamber. The mixture burns here and produces an even hotter gas that turns a set of turbine blades, which work a little like a high-precision windmill.

Turbofan Jet

A turbofan jet engine is a type of gas turbine used to power passenger airliners.

1. The fan draws cool air into the engine.

2. Some of the air passes into the compressor.

3. The compressor is a turbine in reverse. Its spinning wheels squeeze the air, heating it up.

4. Fuel is squirted into the hot air in the combustion chamber. The heat makes the fuel burn.

5. The exhaust gases blast out of the rear nozzle.

6. As they pass, the hot gases spin a turbine.

7. The turbine turns a drive shaft and powers the fan.

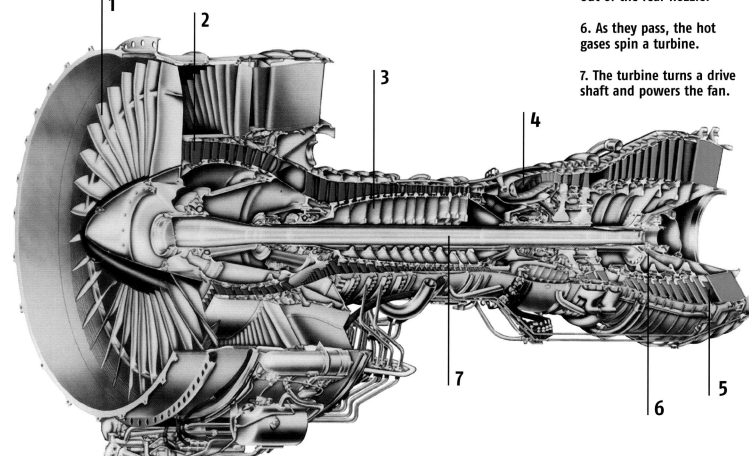

Finally, the hot gases blast out from the exhaust nozzle at the back of the engine.

Gas turbines are used in several different ways. In an airplane, the power of the exhaust gases shooting backward pushes the aircraft forward by the principle of action and reaction. In a ship, the spinning turbine blades drive an electric generator. This generates electricity, which is used to power an electric motor. This, in turn, spins the ship's propeller and moves it through the water.

Rocket engines are simple but powerful. They work by mixing two fuels—an oxidizer and a propellant—in a combustion chamber. The fuels explode when they mix together. The hot exhaust gases are released through a nozzle (above), creating a thrust force.

Rotary Engine

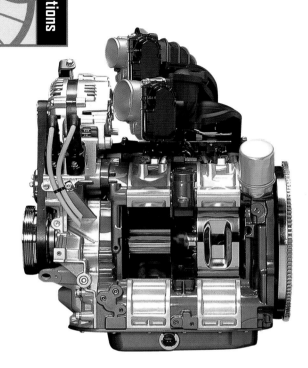

A successful invention can be hard to improve. The internal-combustion engine had changed the world, but in the late 1950s, a German engineer, Dr. Felix Wankel (1902–1988) came up with a new design. Wankel's engine (above) still uses internal combustion but unlike any engine had done before.

Ordinary engines uses a crankshaft to turn the reciprocating (up-and-down) motion of the pistons into rotary motion. The Wankel engine produces rotary motion from the start. It uses an oval-shaped chamber and a metal rotor, which is a triangular shaft with curved edges. The rotor is fitted precisely so it can rotate inside the chamber, just touching the walls. As the rotor turns, it creates three spaces between its edges and the walls of the chamber. Inside these spaces, fuel and air are mixed, burned, and flushed out, much like in an engine with pistons and cylinders. In Wankel's engine, the burning fuel spins the rotor, and this motion drives the car wheels.

This design has many advantages over ordinary engines. It has a third as many moving parts, so it is lighter and less expensive to build. It is also quiet at high speeds, making it good for sports cars. However, it is a complicated job to fit the rotor properly. Although many researched it, few manufacturers chose to power their models with rotary engines when they were invented. By the 1980s, piston engines had become less polluting and were more efficient than the rotary engine.

FOUR STROKES

Four-stroke engines are a type of internal-combustion engine invented in the 1860s. They are so called because the piston inside each cylinder is driven through a series of four strokes—two up strokes, and two down. This process uses fuel much more efficiently than steam power and other previous designs of internal-combustion engine. Since they are so much more efficient, smaller and lighter four-stroke engines can provide the same amount of power as steam engines many times their size and weight.

Several flammable gases and liquids were used to fuel earlier designs of internal-combustion engine. However, the four-stroke engine, built by Nickolaus Otto, was the first to use gasoline as its fuel.

In 1885, Gottlieb Daimler and Karl Benz both used four-stroke engines to power their horseless carriages, or cars. Although improvements have been made since, the engines used in modern cars work in exactly the same way.

Stroke One

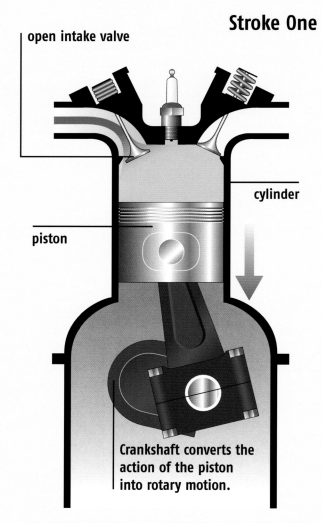

open intake valve

cylinder

piston

Crankshaft converts the action of the piston into rotary motion.

The piston drops. This creates a larger, low-pressure space above the piston. A mixture of air and fuel flows through the open intake valve into the cylinder.

Stroke Two

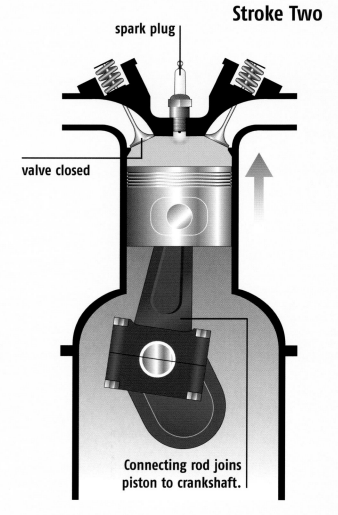

spark plug

valve closed

Connecting rod joins piston to crankshaft.

The piston rises. This squeezes the air-fuel mixture, heating it up. An electric spark from the spark plug sets the fuel alight.

Four-stroke engines have at least four separate cylinders. The largest have 12, which are arranged in a V-shape (right). Smaller engines are in-line with the cylinders arranged in rows. An engine needs four cylinders because only the third stroke is powered by the explosion. The other three strokes need the piston to be pushed or pulled. The force for that comes from the one cylinder in the four that is moving through the third stroke.

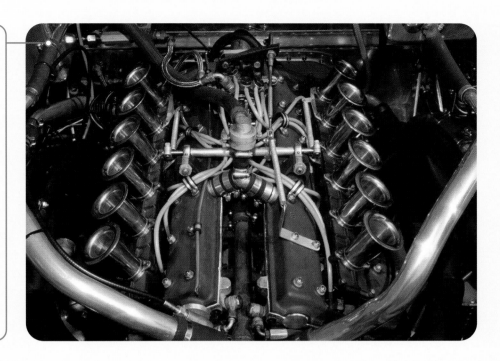

Stroke Three

Stroke Four

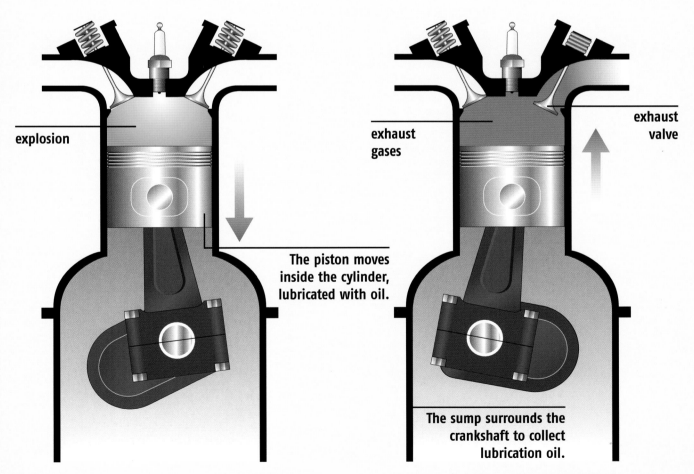

explosion

The piston moves inside the cylinder, lubricated with oil.

exhaust gases

exhaust valve

The sump surrounds the crankshaft to collect lubrication oil.

The fuel explodes. This creates high-pressure exhaust gases. The hot gas forces the piston down again. This stroke powers the engine.

The piston rises for a second time. The exhaust gases produced by the explosion are pushed out of the cylinder, preparing it for stroke one.

THE DAWN OF THE ELECTRIC AGE

A switch sparks as it turns on an electric current. The sparks are caused by the electrical energy heating the air as it jumps between the switch handle and the wall contacts.

Before the invention of devices that harness electricity, people had to produce their own energy. Whether they used windmills or waterwheels, muscle power or steam engines, the energy they needed was always generated near the place where it was used. Electrical technology changed all that by making it possible to produce power in one place and use it in another place, perhaps tens or hundreds of miles away.

THE BIRTH OF ELECTRICITY

When Greek philosopher Thales of Miletus (624–546 B.C.E.) found he could make things electrically charged if he rubbed them with a cloth, he made one of the most important discoveries in the history of civilization. What Thales had stumbled upon was static electricity—the way an electric charge (an amount of electricity) can collect in one place. It is static electricity that gives you an electric shock when you touch a metal object after walking in rubber sneakers. As you touch the metal object, you feel the shock as the electric charge flows away to the ground. The spark that you see is produced as the charge moves from your body to the object. It is similar to lightning although on a much smaller scale.

By the 17th century, people began to understand what static electricity—and electricity as a whole—was all about. At this time, English physician William

How things work

Static Attractions

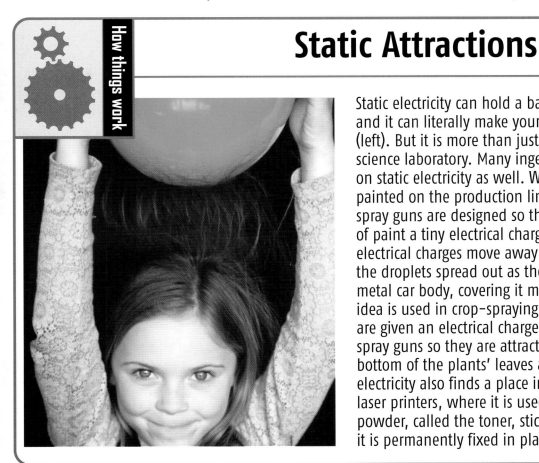

Static electricity can hold a balloon to your sweater, and it can literally make your hair stand on end (left). But it is more than just some fun for the science laboratory. Many ingenious inventions rely on static electricity as well. When automobiles are painted on the production line, for example, the spray guns are designed so they give each droplet of paint a tiny electrical charge. Objects with similar electrical charges move away from one another. So the droplets spread out as they fly toward the metal car body, covering it more evenly. The same idea is used in crop-spraying airplanes. Pesticides are given an electrical charge as they leave the spray guns so they are attracted as much to the bottom of the plants' leaves as to the top. Static electricity also finds a place in photocopiers and laser printers, where it is used to make the ink powder, called the toner, stick to the page before it is permanently fixed in place.

People and society

Ben Franklin's Lightning Conductor

A statesman, publisher, and thinker, Benjamin Franklin lived a very distinguished life. One of the things he is best remembered for is the lightning conductor, which he invented in the 1750s. This is a metal rod that runs down the side of tall buildings, such as churches, to carry lightning bolts harmlessly to Earth.

Franklin had the inspiration for his invention while he was out flying a kite in a thunderstorm. Franklin thought that if the lightning struck his kite, the bolt would travel down the kite string as an electric current. He planned to store the electricity in a large glass and metal jar, known as a capacitor, which he had connected to the lower end of the kite string (left). Fortunately, no lightning struck the kite. If it had done so, Franklin would probably have been killed.

Benjamin Franklin also reasoned that there was only one kind of electricity and not two kinds, as many people before him had believed. He used the words *negative* and *positive* to explain his idea. Negative means that an object has too much electric charge; positive means that it has too little.

Gilbert (1544–1603) suggested that electricity was caused by an invisible fluid called *humor*. If something was rubbed, the humor flowed out of it, and the object became electrically charged. A century later, French scientist Charles du Fay (1698–1739) found that different materials became electrically charged in two different ways. He thought the reason for this was that electricity came in two forms. American statesman and philosopher Benjamin Franklin (1706–90) championed another theory: There was only one kind of electricity and that charged objects had either too much of it (a positive charge) or a lack of it (a negative charge). Both were partly correct. Matter is made of both positively and negatively charged particles, but in most cases it is only the negative electrons that move. Therefore, a positively charged object has a lack of electrons, and a negatively charged one has too many of them.

ELECTRIC CURRENT

Although electricity has many uses when it is static (in one place), it becomes much more useful when it is allowed to move from one place to another. Current electricity, as this is known, is a flow of electricity along a path known as an electrical circuit. When you put a battery in a flashlight, you complete an electrical circuit. This allows a current of electricity to flow around an unbroken loop from the battery into the lamp and back.

Current electricity was stumbled across in 1780. An Italian biology professor called Luigi Galvani (1737–98) was studying how an animal's muscles connected to its nerves. When he hung frog's legs up on a metal hook and touched them with another piece of metal, he found the legs kicked out very briefly, as though they were still alive. Galvani thought some kind of "animal electricity" was being generated inside the frog's legs, and it was this that had caused the eery twitching.

Another Italian scientist, physics professor Alessandro Volta (1745–1827), soon came up with a different explanation. He realized that the frog's legs, the metal hook, the other piece of metal, and Galvani's body made up an electrical circuit. Like all living things, the nerves in Galvani's body produced a small amount of electricity. This electricity flowed

A drawing records the method Italian biologist Luigi Galvini used during his experiment with frogs legs in 1780. Galvini himself did not understand it, but he had created perhaps the first electric circuit.

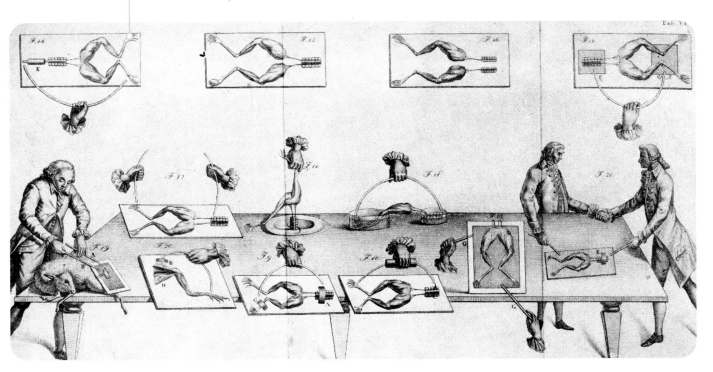

Electrical Energy

Whenever electrical charge accumulates, energy is stored. When an electrical current is allowed to flow, some of the stored energy is released in the form of heat. Lightning (left) provides a dramatic but very common example of electrical energy. As a thundercloud develops, regions of positive and negative charge appear. These are caused by many currents of warm and cold air flowing through the cloud in different directions. When the charge in one region becomes large enough, some of the energy will be released as a current flowing between positive and negative regions inside the cloud or from the cloud to the ground.

Electric current flows whenever there is a "potential difference" of this kind between two objects. The air between the cloud and ground is a very poor conductor so it takes a huge potential to create a current—the lightning. Metal wires are good conductors, however, so they carry currents when the potential is much less. The potential difference of a circuit is also called the voltage.

around the circuit made by the metal items into the dead frog's leg, and it was this that made them kick. Volta's theory was correct, but it proved something else too: It was possible to make electricity by connecting two different metals together with a chemical substance. This discovery led Volta to invent the world's first battery, originally known as a Voltaic pile.

Scientists soon discovered that Volta's primitive battery could be used to power experiments. One of them was a German physicist named Georg Simon Ohm (1789–1854). In 1827, Ohm showed that some materials let electricity flow through them better than others. Metals generally carry electricity very easily. They are said to conduct (carry) electricity well and are known as good conductors. Plastics, wood, and most other nonmetals barely allow electricity to flow through them at all; these poor conductors of electricity are known as insulators. Ohm suggested that conductors have a low resistance to electricity, letting it flow easily, while insulators have a high resistance.

ELECTRICAL ENERGY

Ohm's work paved the way for others to discover the connection between electricity and energy. When electricity flows through a lamp, it gives off light. But it also gives off a great deal of heat. What the lamp is doing is converting electrical energy (the movement of electrons) into light and heat energy. The first person to realize this was James Prescott Joule (1818–98), an Englishman widely regarded as one of the most brilliant physicists of the 19th century. In a series of famous experiments carried out in the 1840s, Joule proved that different types of energy could be changed into one another. This is one of the most important ideas in physics and is known as the conservation of energy. One of these experiments showed how a certain quantity of electricity could be used to produce exactly the same amount of heat. This is the basic principle behind electric heaters, stoves, irons, toasters, coffee pots, and a range of other heating appliances.

ELECTRICITY MEETS MAGNETISM

The 19th century saw physicists begin to understand electricity on a higher level. One of the greatest discoveries they made was that electricity and magnetism were not two separate phenomena, as people had long supposed, but two parts of the same thing. That important breakthrough was made in 1820 by Danish physicist Hans Christian Oersted (1777–1851). Oersted placed a compass near a metal wire and passed an electric current through it. He saw that the magnetic compass needle stopped pointing north and moved briefly to one side. What he had shown was that objects that were electrified were also magnetic.

More exciting discoveries were soon on the way. The year after Oersted's experiment, French mathematician and physicist Andre-Marie Ampere (1775–1836) showed that two parallel electric cables could push one another apart because of the magnetic force between them. Ampere also worked out a detailed theory of electricity and magnetism.

The most important finding of all was that magnetism could be used to produce electricity. This was discovered by British chemist and physicist Michael Faraday (1791–1867) in the 1820s. It was left to another British physicist, James Clerk Maxwell (1831–79), to explain how electricity and magnetism were really two different sides of a single

English scientist Michael Faraday discovered the phenomenon of induction. When a magnet is moved near a wire, the magnet induces an electric current in the wire. This is the basis for electricity generators used in power plants.

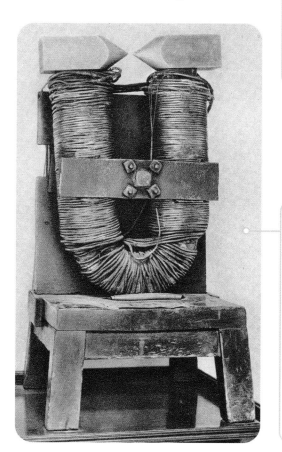

An electromagnet built by Michael Faraday. It was made of an iron core surrounded by a coil of copper wire. This object only became magnetic when an electric current was passed through the wire coil.

Key inventions

Electricity Meets Chemistry

Inside a battery, a chemical reaction is used to generate electricity. In other words, a battery is a device that converts chemical energy into electrical energy. All batteries work in the same way. They have two materials, which make up the positive and negative terminals (or electrodes). An electrolyte, or paste that conducts electricity, permeates both materials.

When a circuit is attached to the terminals, a chemical reaction takes place in the electrolyte that this makes electrons flow around the circuit from the negative terminal to the positive terminal. Even though the current is actually a flow of negatively charged electrons, it is usually described as if it were a flow of positive charge in the other direction, as was originally assumed by Ben Franklin.

A chemical process called electrolysis works like a battery running in reverse. It uses electrical energy from a battery or other power source to make a chemical reaction take place. As a current flows between the two

positive terminal

plastic case

nickel jacket

A mixture of carbon and manganese dioxide makes up the positive electrode.

The negative electrode is made from zinc powder.

A rod made from copper, tin, and zinc collects electrons from the negative electrode.

negative terminal

terminals, chemical changes take place at each electrode. One of the main uses of electrolysis is electroplating, a chemical process that can be used to cover the surface of one metal with another. Electrolysis can also be used to split chemical compounds up. When a current is passed through water, electrolysis generates hydrogen gas and oxygen gas at the two electrodes.

scientific phenomenon called electromagnetism. The connection between electricity and magnetism was more than just interesting science. It led directly to the development of electric motors, devices that use electricity and magnetism to produce motion, and to generators, devices that use mechanical power to generate electric currents. These inventions heralded a new electric age.

ELECTRIC MOTOR

An electric motor is a device that turns electrical energy into mechanical energy. Tiny electric motors spin the disks in DVD players; larger motors turn ship propellers. But no matter how big or small they are, electric motors all rely on the same basic principles of electromagnetism.

If you place a metal wire between the poles of a magnet and connect a battery to its two ends, a current will flow through the completed circuit. Something else will happen, too: The wire will jump up briefly when the battery is connected. The current creates a magnetic field all around the wire, effectively turning it into a temporary magnet. The wire's field pushes against the field of the permanent magnet, and moves away. In this way, electricity and magnetism work together to produce a force.

Now if the current running through the wire continues in the same direction, and the wire is free to move, the wire will be pushed out of the magnetic field. If the current flows through a loop, however, the force acting on the different parts of the loop will create a torque (turning force), causing the loop to

Electric generators from the late 19th century, driven by chain belts running under the floor. Generators are essentially electric motors working in reverse.

rotate until it is parallel to the direction of the magnetic field. If the current were to change direction at this point, the torque would continue to cause the coil to rotate in the same way. A device called a commutator makes it possible for the current to change directions twice every rotation, resulting in a continuing rotation of

Electric Motor

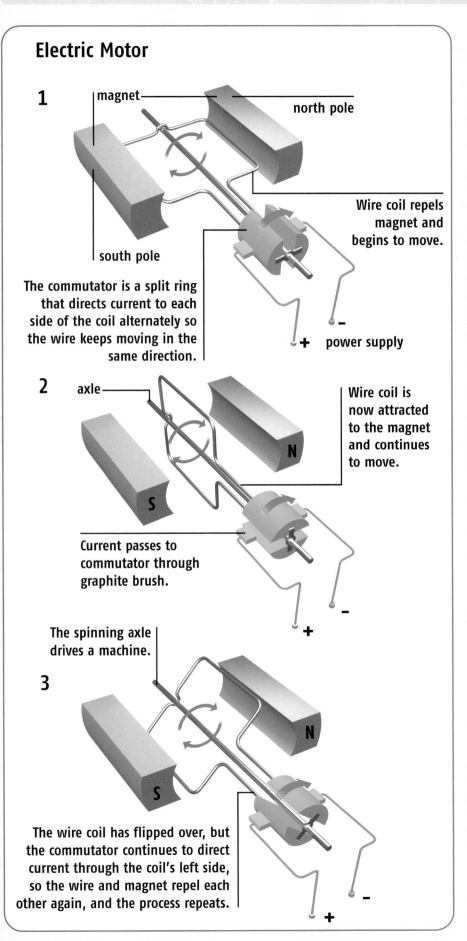

1

magnet — north pole

Wire coil repels magnet and begins to move.

south pole

The commutator is a split ring that directs current to each side of the coil alternately so the wire keeps moving in the same direction.

2

axle

Wire coil is now attracted to the magnet and continues to move.

N

S

Current passes to commutator through graphite brush.

+ power supply

−

+

The spinning axle drives a machine.

3

N

S

The wire coil has flipped over, but the commutator continues to direct current through the coil's left side, so the wire and magnet repel each other again, and the process repeats.

−

+

the coil. As the motor spins, an axle running through its center spins, too, and can be used to drive a machine.

An electric generator works in almost exactly the opposite way to an electric motor. Suppose you take an electric motor and connect it to a bulb rather than a power source. As you spin the motor's axle with your finger, the bulb will light up as a current is generated in the motor's wire coil. The same thing happens in a bicycle dynamo, or an electricity generator in a power plant. As the central axle of the generator spins around, its mechanical energy is converted into electrical energy. This phenomenon is called *induction*. The electric current is induced (made) to flow through the wire as it moves inside a magnetic field.

Both electric motors and generators were invented in the early 19th century. English inventor Michael Faraday built the first electricity generator in the 1820s. The first motors used electromagnets, which only become magnetic when a current flows through them. These were invented by Briton William Sturgeon (1783–1850) and American Joseph Henry (1797–1878). Sturgeon also invented the commutator and designed the world's first successful electric motors in the 1830s.

ELECTRICITY IN THE MODERN WORLD

Electricity is carried around the country in thick cables. Many of these are suspended from pylons, that keep them insulated from the ground so they do not lose power or electrocute people.

Back in the 1820s, Michael Faraday's research had proved that it was possible to generate small amounts of electricity in a laboratory with a simple rotating magnet. But it was another 50 years before generators capable of producing large amounts of power were invented. Belgian engineer Zénobe Gramme (1826–1901) was the first person to make generators of this kind in the 1870s. He also developed the world's first large-scale electric motors at the same time.

Ordinary people began to use electricity a decade later when generators were first used to supply power to towns and industry. The world's first power plant was built in Godalming, England in 1881. An old water mill in the town was connected to an electric generator. It provided enough power to light almost 40 street lamps. The following year, the celebrated American inventor Thomas Alva Edison (1847–1931) built a temporary power plant in

How things work

How Materials Conduct Electricity

metal conductor | Electrons flow from negative to positive.

Convention states that the current flows from positive to negative, the opposite way to the actual flow of electrons.

power supply

+ | -

The internal structure of metal, is arranged in such a way that electrons can drift freely through the whole structure. Normally, the electrons move randomly back and forth. But when a battery or another source of power is connected to the metal, the electrons begin to move in the same direction. Each electron carries a tiny negative charge, and the flow of many electrons through the metal is a bit like ants carrying leaves: Together, the electrons can carry a huge electric current through the metal.

Not all materials behave in this way. In an insulator, the atoms are bound together so that their electrons are not free to move. This is why insulators carry electricity very poorly, if at all. Some materials allow electrons to move through them more easily than others. In other words, they resist an electric current much less. Scientists use the term resistance to describe the difficulty of passing a current through a material. Materials with low resistance, such as metal, allow electrons to flow more easily than those with high resistance, such as plastics.

London, England, followed by the world's first permanent power plant in New York City. The New York Plant, on Pearl Street, produced enough power to light 1,300 lamps.

CONVENIENCE

Edison's plant produced a new and convenient type of power that could be turned on and off with the flick of a switch. However, few people needed to use it. Gas lamps lit their homes and coal fires kept them warm. However, Edison had already invented something that would create a demand for his electricity—the lightbulb.

Once this and other convenient electrical appliances began to be used, the success of electric power was assured. Electric kettles first appeared as long ago as 1893, followed by electric radiators (1894), electric washing machines (1907), dishwashers (1912), toasters (1913), razors (1928), and even electric guitars (1935). By 1941, 80 percent of American homes were connected to the power grid. Almost all of these homes had an electric iron and half owned a vacuum cleaner.

THE ELECTRONIC WORLD

In the last part of the 19th century, Irish physicist George Johnstone Stoney (1826–1911) and German physicist Herman von Helmholtz (1821–94) found a whole new way to understand electricity. They advanced a theory in which electric charge and electric current were caused by tiny electric particles that could build up in one place or move from one place to another. Their radical ideas were confirmed in 1898 by British physicist J. J.

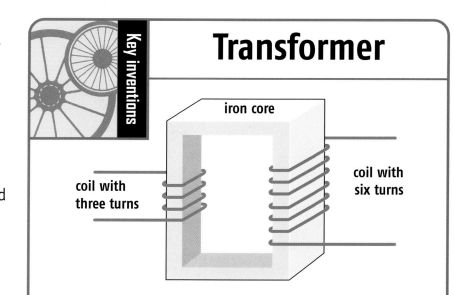

Key inventions

Transformer

iron core

coil with three turns

coil with six turns

A transformer is a device that changes the voltage (potential) of an electric current. It has two wire coils wrapped around an iron core. One coil has more turns than the other. In the example above, a current in the red coil induces another in the blue one with twice the voltage. In the reverse direction, the voltage is halved. Power grids carry high-voltage electricity, much higher than is needed to power appliances in the home. Step-up transformers (below) convert the current made in a power plant to the correct voltage for transmission. Step-down transformers near homes reduce the voltage, making it suitable for powering ordinary appliances.

Thomson (1856–1940). He discovered that atoms contain minute particles called electrons. Further research showed that electricity was a flow of electrons.

The electron theory was of tremendous importance—and not just for scientific reasons. Once inventors found out how to collect and control electrons, they were able to develop a new field of invention called electronics. Early electrical appliances used large currents to work their components, such as lamps or motors. In an electronic appliance, tiny electric currents control how the appliance works, using intricate circuits. Electronic devices proved to be more versatile than basic electric ones. Through the development of such inventions as radio, television, and computers, electronics changed the way people lived forever.

Components

Electronic devices, such as a computer or cell phone, have hundreds if not thousands of tiny components. Each one of these components has a certain job to do that involves handling an electric current in a different way. The components work together in circuits. Each circuit does a different job, such as controlling the sound in a radio or reading a compact disk.

CAPACITOR
A device that stores electric charge to be released when needed.

DIODE
An electrical one-way street: Current can flow through it in one direction only. Diodes that give off light, known as light-emitting diodes or LEDs (right), are used in digital displays.

RESISTOR
A device that adds resistance to a circuit. The volume control in a stereo is a special type of resistor. Its resistance is increased or decreased by turning a knob.

TRANSISTOR
A transistor can be used in two ways: It can switch a current on or off, or it can increase its size. Transistors are used as amplifiers inside radios, where they make faint signals easier to hear. In computers, transistors work as switches.

Tens, hundreds, or thousands of resistors, transistors, capacitors, and other components can be reduced in size and scored onto the surface of a tiny chip of silicon. This is known as an integrated circuit (above). Microprocessors are examples of integrated circuits in which an entire computer is built onto a single silicon chip!

POWER GRID

Generating electric power is not simply a matter of converting energy from fuels, such as coal, into electricity. It is also involves getting electricity from the power plant to the factories, offices, and homes that need it. In countries such as the United States, power plants and transmission lines are connected together to form a huge power distribution network called a grid. This means the electricity you use may have been generated in another state, or even on the opposite side of the country!

Electricity is made in power plants by converting the heat released from burning fuel. All power plants make alternating current (AC) electricity, which is constantly switching direction. Since the current is always rising and falling, AC loses less energy as it is transmitted, making it more economical than unchanging direct current (DC).

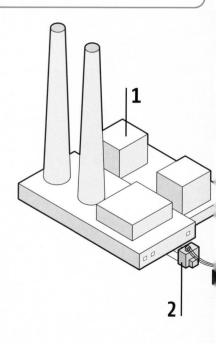

1

2

Power Delivery

1. Power Plant: This converts a fuel, generally coal or gas, into electricity. The fuel is burned to heat water and produce steam. The steam turns a set of turbines, which spin an electricity generator. The large generators used produce electricity at between 1,000 and 26,000 volts.

The volt is the unit of electrical potential. The amount of current that flows through a conductor is proportional to the potential difference, or voltage of the conducting material. At high voltages, an electric current is more likely to flow than at low voltages.

2. Step-Up Transformer: The electricity needs to flow along cables to where it is needed. However, these cables get hot as they carry the current in the same way as an electric heater. A lot of the energy in the electricity can be lost when it is sent over long distances. The amount of energy wasted increases with the size of the current passing through the wires. Less energy is wasted by sending small currents at very high voltages instead of large currents at low voltages.

Step-up transformers at the power plant greatly increase the voltage of the electricity to between 138,000 and 765,000 volts, but in doing so reduces the electric current carried in the cable.

3. Pylons and Cables: The power grid is made up of thousands of miles of cable, suspended from thousands of steel pylons. The cables are made from aluminum, so they not only have a very low resistance but are also very light. Electricity is carried through the cables at enormously high voltages. The cables hang from pylons because this is an inexpensive way of keeping them insulated and out of harm's way. In urban areas, transmission lines are usually buried under the street.

4. Substations: Once the electricity nears its destination, it is reduced to a voltage of between 69,000 and 138,000 volts at step-down transformers in substations.

5. Step-Down Transformers: The voltage is reduced yet further to suit the needs of different users. Factories and electric trains use a supply of several thousand volts, but businesses and homes receive a supply that is about 120 volts.

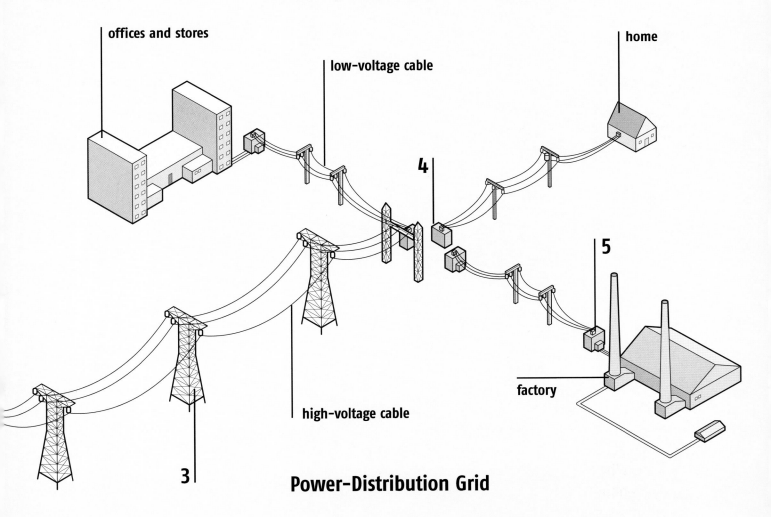

Power-Distribution Grid

ELECTRIC LIGHT

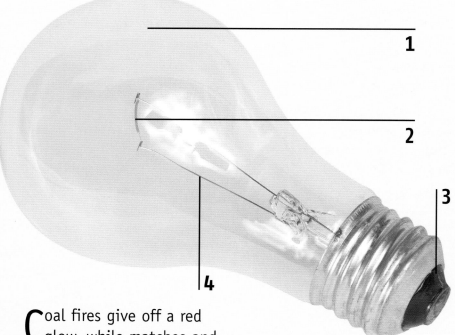

Lightbulb

1. The glass bulb contains unreactive gases that stop the filament from burning away and creating ash.

2. The filament is coiled to make it as long as possible. Longer wires have higher resistance and make brighter light.

3. The contact connects to the power supply through a socket.

4. The wires not only supply the filament with electric current but also provide structural support.

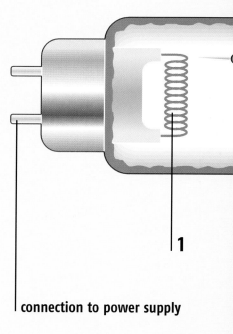

connection to power supply

Coal fires give off a red glow, while matches and candles burn with a yellow-blue flame. When things warm up, they release radiation, including heat and visible light. Incandescence, as this is known, is the scientific phenomenon behind the electric light—perhaps the most successful invention ever developed.

The first electric lights used electricity in a dramatic way. They consisted of two carbon rods that were separated by a tiny gap. A high voltage (difference in electric potential) was then applied to the rods using a powerful battery or generator. When the voltage was high enough, electrons jumped across the gap. This heated the air and the rods to a very high temperature, creating dazzling sparks of electric light. Although arc lights, as these inventions are known, were widely used in the late 19th century, they were never popular. They were too bright and too noisy, and the rods soon disintegrated as the heat vaporized the carbon.

Modern electric lights work in a very different way. Inside a lightbulb, an electric current flows through a long coil of thin metal wire, known as a filament. Being so thin, the wire gets hot very quickly and gives off light and heat through incandescence.

The electric light was first demonstrated in 1847 by Englishman William Staite. The light he developed had a carbon rod encased in a glass bulb. The rod became so hot, however, that it quickly burned up in the air inside the glass.

It took the genius of Thomas Alva Edison (1847–1931), in the United States, and his English rival Joseph Wilson Swan (1828– 1914) to come up with the solution. Instead of using a carbon rod, they made bulbs with a metal filament that would not burn so quickly. At first, Edison and Swan fought each other over the invention, which they both claimed to have developed in the 1870s. Later, the two agreed to join forces. In the decades that followed, their design was improved by using filaments made from dense metals such as osmium and then tungsten.

Despite lasting longer than carbon ones, metal filaments did eventually burn away. In 1913, U.S. chemist Irving Langmuir extended the life of electric bulbs by filling them with argon gas. Argon is very unreactive and stopped the burning that destroyed the filaments. It also prevents bulbs from turning black inside.

Incandescent electric lights produce about 90 percent heat and only about 10 percent light. In other words, they work better as heaters than as lights! Modern fluorescent lights are much more efficient. A fluorescent light is filled with argon and mercury vapor. When electrified, this mixture gives off invisible radiation called ultraviolet light. The light's tube is coated on the inside with a chemical called phosphor. This converts the ultraviolet light into visible light. Fluorescent lights use about 80 percent less energy than incandescent lightbulbs and last 10 times longer.

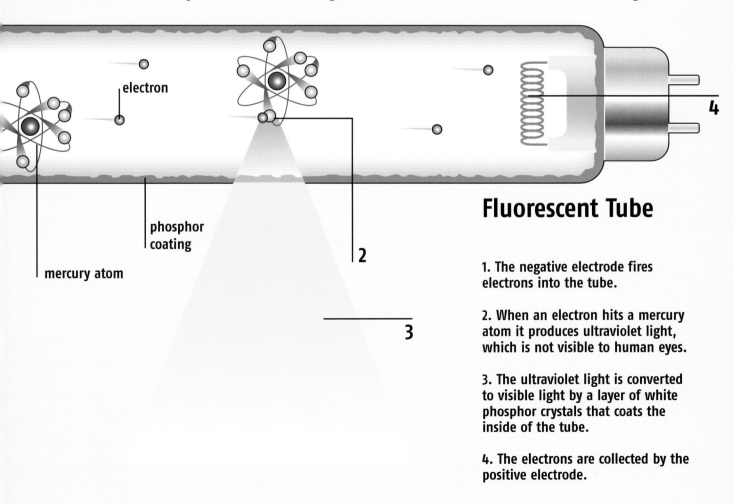

electron

phosphor coating

mercury atom

2

3

4

Fluorescent Tube

1. The negative electrode fires electrons into the tube.

2. When an electron hits a mercury atom it produces ultraviolet light, which is not visible to human eyes.

3. The ultraviolet light is converted to visible light by a layer of white phosphor crystals that coats the inside of the tube.

4. The electrons are collected by the positive electrode.

NUCLEAR POWER

Nuclear power plants look very different to power plants that burn fossil fuels. Instead of having a furnace with tall chimneys, nuclear facilities have super-strong domed concrete buildings that house the reactors.

At the end of the 19th century, the discovery of radioactivity led to a new source of energy that people believed would be almost free to produce in virtually unlimited quantities. However, nuclear power, as this energy became known, had a darker side, too. By the end of the 20th century, the horrifying specter of nuclear war and a number of catastrophic accidents at nuclear power plants had turned this nuclear dream into a nightmare.

RADIOACTIVITY

The nuclear age began in 1896 with momentous discoveries by three French physicists. Antoine-Henri Becquerel (1852–1908), Marie Curie (1867–1934), and her husband Pierre Curie (1859–1906) found that some large and unstable atoms naturally give off radiation (waves of invisible particles) when they decay (break apart) into smaller and more stable atoms. Marie Curie called this new discovery radioactivity and

How things work

Nuclear Fission

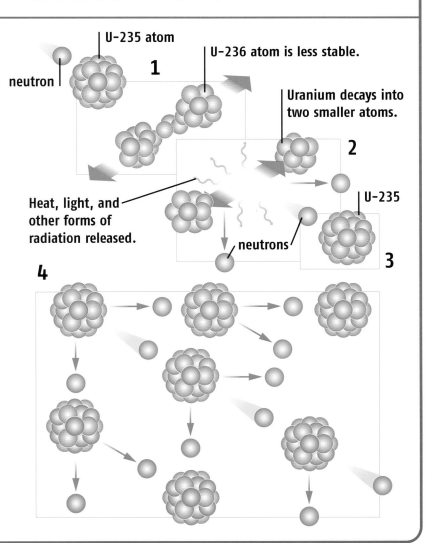

1 — U-235 atom / neutron

U-236 atom is less stable.

Uranium decays into two smaller atoms.

2

Heat, light, and other forms of radiation released.

neutrons

U-235

3

4

Many atoms exist in slightly different forms known as isotopes. Heavy atoms, such as uranium, have isotopes that are more unstable and radioactive than other isotopes. The unstable forms tend to split up into more stable atoms in a process called nuclear fission. A huge amount of energy is produced during nuclear fission. A piece of uranium can generate around two to three million times as much energy as a piece of coal of the same size.

Uranium has thee isotopes. Uranium 238 (U-238) is the most stable, followed by U-235, with U-236 being the most unstable. If a neutron (uncharged atomic particle) is fired at a U-235 atom (1), the U-235 turns into unstable U-236. This splits up, giving off energy, radiation, and more neutrons (2). The neutrons hit other U-235 atoms (3) and this causes a chain reaction—an avalanche of nuclear fission (4).

How things work

Nuclear Fusion

The Sun is a natural nuclear power plant. Unlike the nuclear plants on Earth, which make their energy by the fission of large atoms into small ones, the Sun produces energy by joining small atoms together to make larger ones. This process is called nuclear fusion.

One type of nuclear fusion uses two isotopes of hydrogen: Deuterium has one proton and one neutron, while tritium has one proton and two neutrons (1). At extremely high temperature and pressure (2), deuterium and tritium atoms will fuse together (3) to produce one atom of helium, one neutron, and energy (4).

No one has yet managed to make nuclear fusion work economically because of the huge temperatures and pressures needed. In the 1990s, two physicists thought they had managed to make fusion happen at room temperature. These experiments in "cold fusion" were discounted by most scientists, however, and few people believe such a thing is possible today.

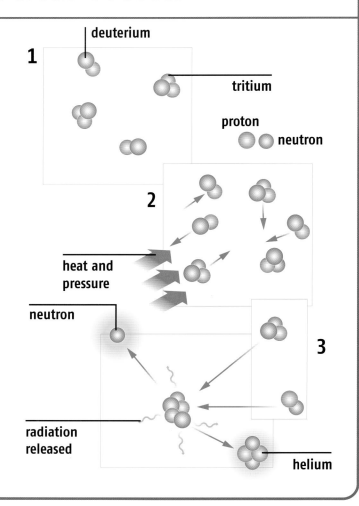

the three French scientists shared the 1903 Nobel Prize for Physics for their work.

What Becquerel and the Curies did not realize was that huge amounts of energy were given off during a decay process, which is called nuclear fission. A fission reaction is sometimes described as "splitting the atom." The source of this energy was eventually explained by another eminent physicist, the German-born American Albert Einstein (1879–1955). Einstein's famous equation $E=mc^2$ states that a small amount of mass (m) can be converted into a huge amount of energy (E). The substances that exist at the start of a fission reaction always have more mass than the chemicals that are left over at the end of it. This small difference in mass is converted into a huge amount of energy during the nuclear reaction.

NUCLEAR POWER

Einstein was a pacifist, but his work soon opened the door to the most terrifying weapon ever produced—the nuclear bomb. That invention became possible after an important discovery by Italian physicist Enrico Fermi (1901–54), who was working in the United States. In 1942, Fermi proved that a single fission reaction could trigger others, which would trigger still more, and so on. This nuclear "chain reaction" would continue indefinitely, generating a huge amount of energy as it did so. Few people understood what Fermi had discovered until August 1945, when U.S. planes dropped nuclear bombs on the Japanese cities of Hiroshima and Nagasaki. Up to 150,000 people were killed and huge areas of both cities were ruined, but the attacks brought World War II to an end.

The development of nuclear weapons terrified and appalled many people, but it had a very important spin-off. Nuclear bombs use a radioactive metal called plutonium, which has to be made from uranium, another radioactive metal. During the 1940s, American scientists built nuclear reactors in remote parts of Washington and South Carolina. Nuclear reactions were controlled inside the reactors to produce plutonium. They also produced heat that, at first, was simply wasted. Eventually scientists realized they could use this heat to generate electricity.

By the 1950s, the United States, and several other countries were developing nuclear power. The world's first nuclear power plant was opened in northwest England in 1956. Originally known as Calder Hall, it was later renamed Sellafield and remains one of the world's most important nuclear

The work of Albert Einstein explained how radioactive material could release huge amounts of energy. His ideas were put into practice to make nuclear bombs. These weapons are the most powerful ever made. The bombs produce a cloud shaped like a mushroom when they explode.

plants. The first U.S. plant opened at Shippingport, Pennsylvania in 1957. Nuclear energy expanded rapidly in the years that followed. The United States currently has 104 nuclear reactors used for producing energy and 36 other reactors used for making nuclear weapons and for research.

NUCLEAR NIGHTMARES?

Far from the promise of inexpensive energy, nuclear plants proved expensive to operate. Minor technical problems posed a major safety risk, while major incidents could turn nuclear plants into nothing less than nuclear bombs. In 1952, Canada's first reactor at Chalk River, Ontario, began to "melt down," or become too hot. A large amount of radioactive water escaped from the reactor. In Britain, radiation was spread over a wide area after a major fire in the Windscale reactor in 1957. The United States experienced its most serious nuclear accident in 1979. More than 100,000 people had to be evacuated from around the Three Mile Island site at Harrisburg, Pennsylvania, after a series of mistakes led to a partial meltdown. The accident cost around $1 billion to clean up.

The world's worst nuclear disaster to date happened at Chernobyl, Ukraine, in 1986. An explosion in one of the plant's reactors killed 31 people and threw a cloud of fallout (radioactive dust) more than 1 mile (1.6 km) into the sky. A lot of the fallout settled over a vast area around the plant, but some of it was also blown by the wind across much of Europe. Over the next few days, radioactive rain fell on several countries. Tens of thousands of people are expected to eventually die of cancer and other diseases caused by the radiation released at Chernobyl.

The accident badly shook the world's confidence in nuclear power, and some countries immediately cancelled plans to build nuclear plants. Interest began to turn to safer kinds of power, including renewable energy, that would be less harmful to the environment.

Nuclear Waste

People and society

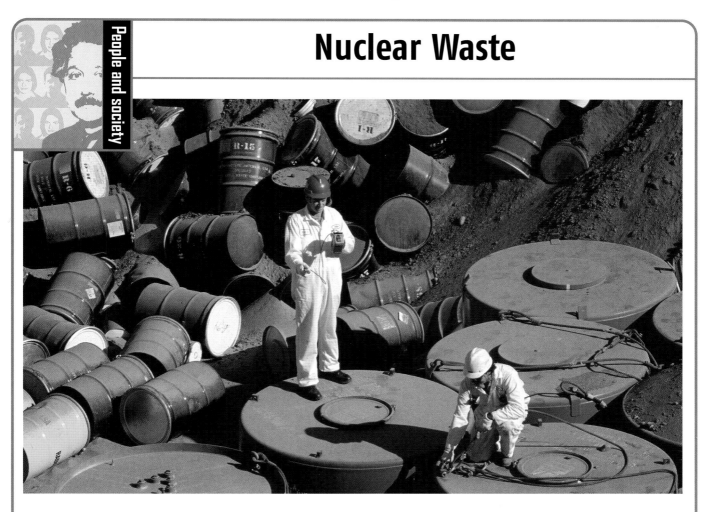

One of the biggest drawbacks of nuclear power plants is the waste they produce. This waste can remain radioactive for many thousands of years. Although it is relatively easy to store nuclear waste in barrels (above) or sealed in materials such as glass and concrete, most people oppose having nuclear waste buried anywhere near them. Even burial at sea has proved controversial, because no one can be sure that radiation will not leak out and contaminate fish stocks or eventually travel

back to land. Waste leaking from nuclear plants has caused problems before. Traces of radioactive waste from Britain's Sellafield plant have been found on the coasts of Norway, Denmark, Greenland, Siberia in Russia, and even under the ice at the North Pole. Sellafield extracts unused fuel from nuclear waste for many other countries. This shows that nuclear pollution can pose a serious threat not just to the area around a nuclear plant but to the entire global environment.

NUCLEAR REACTOR

The core of a nuclear reactor is opened for refueling. For safety, the reactor is covered by a pool of water. This prevents radiation from leaking out.

Although nuclear plants may seem highly complex, they convert heat energy into mechanical and electrical power in much the same way as any other power plant. The main difference is that the heat comes from nuclear reactions, which take place in a reactor, the part of a nuclear power plant where energy is released.

The reactor contains four main components: the fuel, the moderator, the control rods, and the cooling fluid. The fuel comes in solid rods made from uranium dioxide, which are placed inside the reactor core. The moderator is usually made from graphite. Its job is to slow down the neutrons produced during nuclear fission. This increases the chance of their colliding with more uranium atoms and ensures that the chain reaction of atomic collisions continues. However, the reaction cannot be allowed to run out of control. A set of control rods made from cadmium metal or boron are used to slow the reaction if needed. These rods absorb neutrons and reduce the number of fissions taking place in the reactor. The rods are lowered into the reactor to make the reactor release energy more slowly. Raising them again speeds up the reaction. If the reactor runs too quickly, it can overheat or even explode. This situation is known as a meltdown.

There is one more essential component in the reactor: the cooling fluid, sometimes also called the coolant. This is pumped around the reactor to remove the heat produced during the nuclear reactions. It enters the reactor cold, heats up and then leaves the reactor extremely hot. The hot cooling fluid is used to boil water and make steam in a device known as a heat exchanger. This steam is used to drive a turbine, which turns a generator and makes electricity in much the same way as any other power plant.

Most U.S. plants use water as a coolant, while those in other countries use gas. Many water-cooled plants keep the coolant under high pressure, a design known as a pressurized water reactor (PWR). Another design called a boiling water reactor (BWR) uses water at lower pressure as the cooling fluid. As the water pumps around the reactor, it boils and turns to steam. The steam is used to turn a turbine directly, so there is no need for a heat exchanger, and less energy is wasted.

Breeder reactors also work by nuclear fission, but use a different isotope of uranium as their fuel. They are called breeder reactors because they generate more fuel as well as energy. Another product of breeder reactors is plutonium, which is used in weapons.

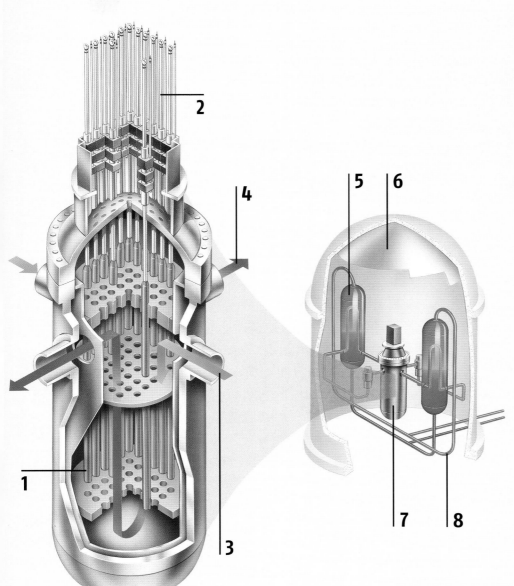

Nuclear Reactor

Nuclear reactor cores are built inside pressure vessels that keep the radiation and heat safely inside.

1. Bundles of uranium rods are loaded into a fuel assembly, with space left inside for control rods.

2. Control rods can be moved in and out of each assembly.

3. Cold water is pumped at high pressure into the space between the fuel assemblies, where it begins to heat up.

4. Hot water leaves the reactor and travels to a heat exchanger.

5. The water coolant from the reactor is used to heat more water inside the exchangers

6. The reactor and exchangers are contained inside a steel and concrete dome.

7. The reactor core has a thick steel jacket.

8. The water heated in the exchangers is used to drive turbines and make electricity.

RENEWABLE ENERGY

Earth's supplies of fossil fuels may seem huge, but they are not unlimited. Even if those fuels lasted forever, problems with the environment, such as global warming and pollution, are also forcing people to look for other sources of energy. Renewable energy, so-called because it will never run out, uses natural power sources, such as sunlight, wind, and tides. A fifth of the world's energy comes from these sources.

One of the advantages of renewable energy is that it does not need to be generated on a large scale and transmitted over a grid system like electricity made from fossil fuels. Solar panels can be used to make electricity and water just for one home. A small community can invest in its own wind turbine just to produce power for the local area. In practice, renewable schemes of this kind are often still connected to the main power grid. When demand for electricity is low, they can sell their energy to the grid for use in other places. In effect, this means the community runs its own mini-power plant.

Solar power plants are very expensive to build but create large amounts of electricity directly from sunlight. The solar panels used are either arranged to catch as much light as possible, as above, or have small motors that keep them pointing straight at the Sun.

SOLAR POWER

Nearly all of our energy comes from the Sun. Even fuels like coal and oil store energy that originally arrived as sunlight. Solar power involves making energy directly from sunlight in one of three ways. Buildings can be designed with large areas of glass so they heat up naturally in daytime; this is known as passive solar energy. In another design, known as active solar, large black solar panels can be fastened to the roof of any existing building. Water is pumped constantly through the panels from a tank. This water is heated up by the sunlight as it moves through. This type of solar power reduces the cost of running a normal hot water system. A third type of solar energy is called solar electric. This uses a different type of solar panel made from photovoltaic cells. These cells are made from materials that convert light into electricity. Solar cells of this kind were first built by Charles Fritts in 1899, but they were very inefficient. Fritts' cells converted only 1 percent of the incoming solar energy into electricity. Modern solar cells made of layers of silicon were invented by Russell Ohl in 1941 and are much more efficient.

WIND POWER

Modern wind turbines are also more efficient than earlier windmills. The most common designs look a bit like gigantic airplane propellers mounted on high towers. The first wind turbine of this kind was tested on a hillside at Grandpa's Knob in Rutland, Vermont, in the 1940s. By the 1980s, generous tax concessions in states such as California had led to the creation of *wind farms* with tens or even hundreds of turbines. In windy countries with large areas of coastline, such as Britain, interest is now turning to offshore wind farms. Being less sheltered from the wind than wind farms on land,

Key inventions

Fuel Cells

One day cars might produce nothing more polluting than water. These cars will be powered by fuel-cell engines (above). A fuel cell is like a battery, because it makes electrical energy from chemical reactions. Instead of gradually using up the chemicals inside it to make energy, like a battery does, a fuel cell uses a continuous supply of fuel. The fuel is usually hydrogen gas, which is pumped in from a tank. This gas combines with the oxygen in the air to make water vapor, or steam. The fuel cell make use of an electric current produced by the chemical reaction.

Wind turbines are excellent ways of making electricity when the wind is blowing. However, when the wind drops, the turbines become useless. They are also damaged by high winds.

these turbines can generate much more energy—and they would be less unsightly too.

BIOMASS

Biomass fuels are those produced from organic materials, generally plants or dung. They currently supply around 15 percent of the world's total energy, and they are by far the main source of energy in developing countries. Biomass has also recently become more common in developed countries, too, where crops are now being grown specially for burning in highly efficient power plants. The main advantage of biomass fuels is that they does not add to the problem of global warming, as do fossil fuels. The carbon dioxide given off when a tree burns is the same as the carbon dioxide the tree takes in when it grows. So if trees are grown specially for burning, no overall carbon dioxide is produced.

Many biomass power plants have now been built worldwide. The largest one, at Pietarsaari, Finland, runs on bales of waste products from the nearby forestry industry. Other biomass plants burn different kinds of plants. The town of Ely, England, is home to the world's largest straw-burning

Sea Power

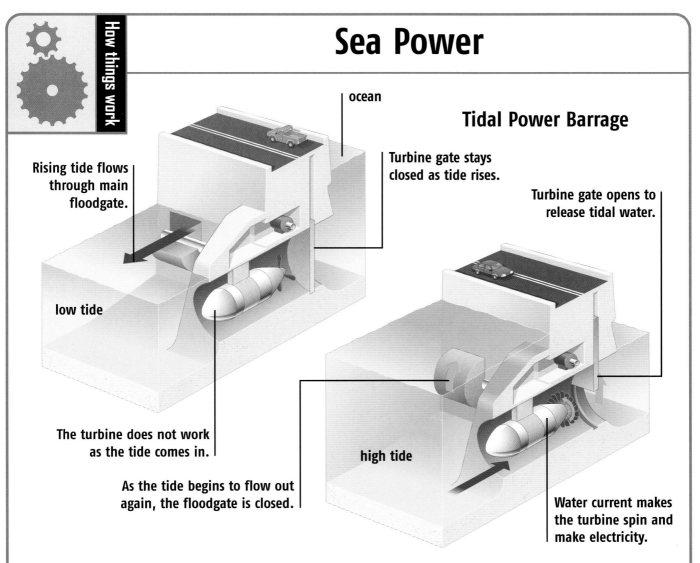

Tidal Power Barrage

ocean

Rising tide flows through main floodgate.

Turbine gate stays closed as tide rises.

Turbine gate opens to release tidal water.

low tide

The turbine does not work as the tide comes in.

As the tide begins to flow out again, the floodgate is closed.

high tide

Water current makes the turbine spin and make electricity.

Inventors have long tried to harness the immense amount of energy locked in the oceans, but with only limited success. The tides, the waves, and the heat energy stored in seawater can all be used to make power. However, the ocean can be a very harsh environment, making it a much tougher place to generate power than dry land.

Tidal power systems usually take the form of large barrages, or dams, across river mouths. As the tides flood in and out of the river, the water flows through turbines and generates electricity (above). The world's best-known tidal power plant was built at the mouth of the La Rance River in France in 1966. The facility still operates today.

Wave-power systems attempt to turn the up-and-down motion of the ocean's waves into useful electricity. Some devices, such as Salter's ducks, sit on the waves and generate electricity as they rock up and down. Another design known as an oscillating water column (OWC) can either be built on the coastline or fitted to a stationary ship. As the waves wash past, rising up and down, a column of water inside the OWC pushes air up and down a shaft. The moving air turns a small wind turbine and generates electricity.

Electricity can also be made by harnessing the temperature difference between the surface of the ocean, where the water is warm, and its depths, where the water is much cooler. This technique is known as ocean thermal energy conversion (OTEC) and has the potential to generate enormous amounts of energy. Unlike other types of ocean power, which typically use turbines to make electricity, OTEC plants are heat engines. This means they are quite inefficient at converting energy, and they need to be very large as a result.

plant. During the 1980s, the U.S. government ran a research program called Ocean Food and Energy Farm (OFEF) to investigate making biomass fuel from sea plants. In the United States, biomass energy is already produced at almost 350 small plants and makes about one percent of the nation's power. It is expected to be the fastest-growing source of renewable energy for the next 20 years.

GEOTHERMAL ENERGY

If you have ever seen Old Faithful, the giant geyser in Yellowstone National Park, you will have an idea of how much heat is trapped inside Earth. This type of natural heat, known as geothermal energy, comes not from the Sun, but from nuclear reactions that happen deep inside Earth's core. In effect, the planet works like a nuclear power plant: Heat is produced inside the solid

Bathers enjoy a swim in the naturally hot spring waters of Iceland's Blue Lagoon. In the background a geothermal power plant taps the heat from the lagoon to make electricity.

Gasohol and Biodiesel

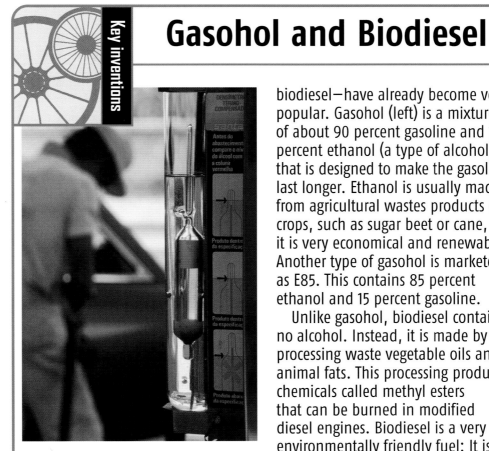

One solution to the world's falling supplies of oil could be to run vehicles on other liquid fuels. Two alternative fuels—gasohol and biodiesel—have already become very popular. Gasohol (left) is a mixture of about 90 percent gasoline and 10 percent ethanol (a type of alcohol) that is designed to make the gasoline last longer. Ethanol is usually made from agricultural wastes products or crops, such as sugar beet or cane, so it is very economical and renewable. Another type of gasohol is marketed as E85. This contains 85 percent ethanol and 15 percent gasoline.

Unlike gasohol, biodiesel contains no alcohol. Instead, it is made by processing waste vegetable oils and animal fats. This processing produces chemicals called methyl esters that can be burned in modified diesel engines. Biodiesel is a very environmentally friendly fuel: It is nontoxic, breaks down naturally in the environment, and produces virtually no harmful pollutants when burned.

metal core and carried up to the surface by convection currents in the magma (melted rocks) deep underground. In a geothermal power plant, cold water is pumped into the ground and returns to the surface as hot water or steam. Hot water is pumped directly to heat homes, while steam is used to make electricity in the usual way. California is home to the world's biggest geothermal power plant, known as The Geysers. It generates enough to power 14 million light bulbs—or the entire metropolitan area of San Francisco.

BACK TO THE FUTURE?

It took our ancestors millions of years to invent simple tools and thousands more years after that to harness the power of nature. In the last 200 years or so, people have turned away from natural power sources in favor of oil, coal, and other fossil fuels. Today, as environmental problems become more acute, people are beginning to understand the true costs of producing power. In the future each home may have its own micro-power plant or receive electricity from several sources.

HYDROELECTRICITY

About 6 percent of the world's renewable energy comes from hydroelectricity. The word *hydroelectricity* means "electricity from water." It is made by blocking the path of a large river with a dam, so the water has to flow through a power-generating turbine. The two main components of a hydroelectric plant are the dam and the turbine.

THE DAM

When a river is blocked with a dam, an enormous volume of water soon builds up behind it. Dams are constructed across large valleys where the water collects to make a gigantic lake or reservoir. The pressure of the water is immense, so dams have to be extremely strong. Dams are strengthened in two different ways. Gravity dams are built out of very broad piles of earth, rock, or concrete and

The water flowing through this dam is spinning turbines that make electricity. Most dams have power plants inside, but many were built for other reasons, such as for controlling floods or collecting irrigation water.

Gravity Dam

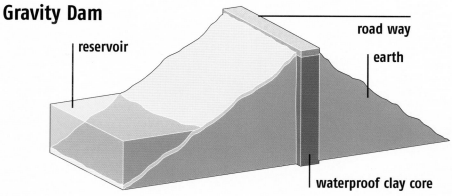

reservoir

road way

earth

waterproof clay core

rely on their weight to stop the water from escaping. Arch dams use a strong concrete arch to span the river valley. Like the arches in a building or bridge, an arch dam transmits the weight of the reservoir's water to the rocks in the river valley. It is these natural rocks, rather than the concrete itself, that provide much of the dam's strength.

THE TURBINE

Although the dam holds back most of the water, some is allowed to escape to the river on the other side through a channel called a penstock. This directs the water past one or more huge turbines that spin around and turn the movement of the water into electricity. Different types of turbines work best according to how high the dam is and the rate at which the water flows through the dam. The Kaplan turbine is like an upside-down propeller. It works best with low dams and high flow rates. Another design known as a Pelton wheel has small buckets attached to a wheel that spins around a horizontal

Grand Coulee Dam

The Grand Coulee Dam on the Columbia River in Washington State is the largest U.S. hydroelectric plant and the third largest electricity producer in the world. The original dam was completed in 1942 and took nine years to build. It is 46 stories high and nearly a mile (1.6 km) wide. The dam contains enough concrete to build a highway 60 feet (18 m) wide and 4 inches (10 cm) thick all the way from Los Angeles to New York City.

Grand Coulee dam generates 6,180,000 million watts of electricity. This may be a vast amount of energy, but it is still a tiny fraction of the electricity people use every day. It would take about 1,500 Grand Coulee Dams to supply all of Earth's electricity!

Kaplan Turbine

control gate

reservoir

axle

turbine

water current

dam

electricity generator

axle. It is used for very high dams and is up to 90 percent efficient—it turns nine-tenths of the water's energy into a current of electricity.

The world's first hydroelectric plant was built at Appleton, Wisconsin, in 1882. A great number of huge dams have been built in the United States and around the world since then. Norway, with its many mountains, and Brazil, with its huge rivers, make almost all of their electricity supply using dams.

Time Line

3500 B.C.E.
The wheel is invented.

600 B.C.E.
Thales of Miletus discovers electricity.

62
Hero of Alexandria describes the five basic machines and invents steam power.

600
Windmills are invented in Persia.

1642
Blaise Pascal invents the first gear-driven calculator.

1780
Luigi Galvani and Alessandro Volta discover current electricity.

1860
Jean Lenoir develops the first practical internal-combustion engine.

c.3500 B.C.E.   600 C.E.   1600   1800

27 C.E.
Roman architect Vitruvius invents the modern water wheel.

400 B.C.E.
Gears are invented in ancient Greece.

1830s
William Sturgeon invents the electric motor.

1820
Hans Christian Oersted discovers electromagnetism.

1698
Thomas Savery builds the first working steam engine.

1867
Nikolaus August
Otto invents the
four-stroke engine.

1885
Rudolf Diesel
invents the
diesel engine.

1990s
Wind turbines and other
forms of renewable power
generation become common.

1870s
Zènobe T. Gramme
develops the first
large-scale electric
generators.

1896
Radioactivity is
discovered by
Henri Becquerel,
Marie Curie, and
Pierre Curie.

2003
World's largest dam
begins generating
power in China.

1900

2000

1882
Thomas Alva Edison
constructs the world's
first power plants.

1986
The Chernobyl nuclear
plant explodes in
the Ukraine.

1879
Joseph Wilson
Swan and
Thomas Alva
Edison invent
the lightbulb.

1956
The world's first nuclear
power plant is built in
the United Kingdom.

1942
Enrico Fermi
demonstrates
the nuclear
chain reaction.

Glossary

cam An egg-shaped wheel that converts rotational motion into reciprocating motion.

chemical energy The energy stored in chemical form in something like a battery.

combustion The process of burning fuel in air to produce energy.

current electricity A type of electricity that flows around a closed path called a circuit.

crankshaft and connecting rod An elbow-shaped pair of levers that converts rotational motion into reciprocating motion.

cylinder The closed compartment in an engine where fuel is burned.

diesel engine An engine that burns heavy oil at high pressures.

dynamo A machine that turns rotational motion into electricity. Also known as a generator.

electrolysis A way of making a chemical reaction happen using electricity.

electronics A type of electricity that can control an electrical appliance or process information.

energy The ability to do work.

engine A machine that converts energy from one form into another.

external combustion An engine that burns the fuel outside of the cylinder.

force A pushing or pulling action.

fuel A substance that can be burned to generate energy.

gear A pair of toothed wheels that increases the speed or power of rotational motion.

generator A machine that turns rotational motion into electricity. Also known as a dynamo.

heat engine An engine that converts heat energy into mechanical work.

hydrocarbon A compound made from hydrogen and carbon

hydroelectricity Electric power produced by damming a river.

machine A device that changes the size or direction of a force.

motor A machine that converts electricity into rotational motion.

potential energy The ability to do work at some time in the future.

pressure The force acting over a certain surface area.

radioactivity The particles or rays given off from unstable atoms.

static electricity A buildup of electricity in one place.

turbine A device that converts the flow of a fluid into rotation.

work A force act over a distance.

Further Resources

Books

Power With Nature: Solar and Wind Energy Demystified by Rex A. Ewing. PixyJack Press LLC, 2003.

Teach Yourself Electricity and Electronics by Stan Gibilisco. McGraw-Hill, 2001.

Web Sites

Smithsonian: Industry, Machines, and Electricity

http://www.si.edu/science_and_technology/industry_machines_and_electricity/

U.S. Department of Energy

http://www.energy.gov/

Index

Picture Credits